Dezeen Book of Interviews

Edited by Marcus Fairs

Published by Dezeen

Dezeen Book of Interviews
Edited by Marcus Fairs

Published by Dezeen Limited

First published in 2014
by Dezeen Limited.
www.dezeenbooks.com

Editor: Marcus Fairs
Production editor: Ben Hobson
Sub editor: Ellen Himelfarb
Editorial assistant: Grace Quah
Design: Micha Weidmann Studio
Interviewers: Claire Barrett,
Rose Etherington, Marcus Fairs,
Amy Frearson, Ben Hobson,
Dan Howarth, James Pallister

A catalogue record for this book is
available from the British Library.

Printed in the UK by Butler Tanner
and Dennis Ltd, Frome and London

Trade orders: Dezeen Limited,
office@dezeen.com
www.dezeenbooks.com

ISBN 978-0-9928474-0-1

Contents

Introduction

by Marcus Fairs

Dezeen is a website about design and architecture but at the end of the day, people are more interesting than objects and buildings.

Since we launched the site in 2006 we've interviewed many of the most talented, inspiring people from the global design scene.

Following the success of our last book, Dezeen Book of Ideas, we thought it would be a good idea to bring the best of these interviews together in a new publication.

Most of the interviews gathered here have been published online, in video, podcast or text format. But we've re-edited them all and included a lot of material that has never been published before.

The only problem was deciding which to include. The 45 we've selected represent a fraction of the conversations we've had, with more than enough left over for a sequel.

But if you can't wait for Dezeen Book of Interviews 2, you can read more at dezeen.com/interviews.

Marcus Fairs is founder and editor-in-chief of Dezeen

There are 45 interviews in this book, conducted on four different continents around the world between 2008 and 2014. Seven of them were conducted as part of Dezeen and MINI World Tour, which saw us visit eight different cities during 2013. You can see these interviews on pages 36, 48, 52, 62, 80, 98 and 154. Interviews with architects appear on pages 18, 40, 48, 74, 94, 104, 122, 148, 158, 168 and 188. Interviews with designers can be found on pages 8, 14, 22, 32, 36, 44, 52, 58, 68, 80, 84, 86, 90, 102, 106, 110, 114, 116, 132, 134, 138, 154, 162, 164, 180, 184 and 198. The remaining conversations involve an eclectic mix of artists, gallerists, curators, entrepreneurs, musicians and more.

deze en book of inter views

Ron Arad
'The Rover chair sucked me into the world of design. I dread to think what it diverted me from'

To coincide with a retrospective of his work at the Barbican in London, the Israeli designer told us how his career began with the chance discovery of a car seat in a scrapyard.

Marcus Fairs You've had retrospective exhibitions in New York and Paris. How does the Barbican show differ?

Ron Arad One thing I don't like about retrospectives is that your life becomes a career. It's not a career. We go to the playground every Monday and interests shift and we get excited by something for a while and then we get excited about something else. If you want to call that a career, then okay, call it a career. It's more to do with getting away with things you like and not worrying about a career. I said before that we're more interested in doing new work, in showing new work, but having shows like at the MoMA in New York and the Centre Pompidou and the Barbican has its rewards and its magic moments.

My Tinker chairs, for example, are early welded pieces that were made by taking thin sheet steel, bending it and hammering it with a rubber mallet, welding it, sitting on it and deciding that bashing this or that a bit more will make it more comfortable. It's the nearest you can get to action painting in design.

What amuses me a lot is that this here is the Rover chair that normally sits in my living room. It came to my home before my daughters were born. They grew up, lived with it, jumped on it, all their friends jumped on it, never taking too much care of it. Then, at the Centre Pompidou, I wasn't permitted to touch it without white gloves. That is another sort of completion of the cycle.

MF Which pieces of your work will be in the Barbican show?

RA This Rover chair will be there and stuff of the same period that relied, more or less, on ready-made and found objects that were not ideology but necessity. I didn't have the industry behind me. I didn't know the industry existed at the time. It was something to do to keep me off the streets. Actually I had to go to the streets to find the stuff. It's not that I was a recycler, although the Rover chair was on the cover of the Friends of the Earth magazine. I'm happy about that, but that wasn't the starting point. If my activity was underpinned by anything, it was more to do with Picasso's Bull's Head[1] and Duchamp's Fountain[2] than with saving the planet.

You can't stay primitive for that long. You get better and better technically. When we thought we had a business in fabricating and making things in metal, just as we got good with it, I decided

Name
Ron Arad
Occupation
Industrial
designer
Location
His studio,
London
Date
February 2010

MAGIC
MOMENTS.

to stop, because I didn't want to become a craftsman. I didn't want to be, like, a fantastic glassblower or a potter on a potter's wheel. I don't have the temperament or the patience of a craftsman. So we subbed out the production to Italy and disbanded the workshop.

A similar thing happened at the height of the Rover chair's success. We decided to stop it because we didn't want to become a Rover chair shop. We cleared out the last 100 Rover chairs because it wasn't an exciting life to be in charge of production. It was exciting, initially, to go to the scrapyards and collect all the Rover seats and take them to this motor trimmer down the road in Kentish Town, which stopped taking any other motor-trimming work other than Rover chairs. So in the same way, when we got really good at making stuff, I stopped it and let the Italians do it.

Above
Ron Arad's
Rover chair, made
from a salvaged
car seat

Ron Arad   The only problem is that they did things more perfectly than us. I enjoy the fact that my own work is not perfect and slightly rough. But the Italian Fish chair I'm sitting on here is an authorised fake. It's named after Gaetano Pesce. This is made in Italy. It's too good. Italian craftsmanship is better than ours. For some pieces it works and with other pieces we prefer the old ones. And collectors will only buy pieces that are made down here in the office.

MF   Is a lot of your work driven by chance discoveries of materials or processes?

RA   In the last century, we discovered rapid prototyping, which was sort of like science fiction. I started playing with it. We did an exhibition in Milan called Not Made by Hand, Not Made in China and it was, I believe, the first time that digital manufacturing was shown as the final pieces, not as the prototyping. We did lights and vases as the final product. It was very exciting until it became commonplace and it has been used and abused by lots of other people since. So there's some of that here.

Sometimes you hit upon a process, like the vacuum forming of aluminium, and it makes you think, 'What can be done with this?' When I was commissioned to do a totem for Milan by the magazine Domus, my totem was made out of a hundred stacking chairs made in vacuum-formed aluminium, which is a process used almost solely in the aerospace industry. We developed the Tom Vac chair with it. The name comes from the fact that it's vacuum formed. And also there is a photographer in Milan called Tom Vack, who is still very active. Whenever he goes to a bar people ask him, 'Are you named after the chair?' It's the other way around, though.

Later we did an industrial version of the piece with Vitra, which became a bestselling piece and was copied in China. I know about 14 factories in China that make the Tom Vac chair, and the way it started was with curiosity about the process. Then we discovered a factory in Worcester where they do deep vacuum forming. They inflate it and then suck it – it avoids wrinkles. Then I became fascinated by the blowing of the aluminium and I said, 'What if the frames through which we blow this are not square but shaped?' And that led to a heap of work. There was a fascination with this amazing process that is a kind of hybrid between the will of the designer and the will of the material.

Like with everything else, we get better and better at it, we get more perfectionist and more demanding, enhancing the materials and the process and the properties of the material. This aluminium is very rich in magnesium, so it polishes more like stainless steel than aluminium and you can indeed do things with it that you could not do otherwise. But at some point you look at it and say, 'I don't want to do any more rocking chairs

or polished pieces.' And then you will do not only things that are back to front but also side to side, just to prove that you can keep your word after you declare that you don't want to do more.

MF What is the most recent of your works in the exhibition?

RA There's Rod Gomli – it's a piece that's loosely named after artist Antony Gormley[3], but spelled differently. It's based on the human figure. But it's everyman. It's not just one person. When you design chairs, you always cater to an invisible sitter who can be male, female, big, small, young, old. Everyone should be happy in it. I started to search for what the figure looks like, the invisible sitter.

MF Is it actually modelled on Antony Gormley?

RA No, I talked to Antony about it and I have a really nice picture of Antony sitting in the Gomli. It's the opposite because Antony's

Above
Ron Arad's
Tom Vac chair

11

Ron Arad

1 Bull's Head is
a sculpture by
Pablo Picasso,
created in 1942
from the seat
and handlebars
of a bicycle

2 Marcel
Duchamp's 1917
artwork Fountain
consisted of a
porcelain urinal,
which was signed
'R.Mutt'

3 Antony Gormley
is a British artist
who has created
numerous cast
iron sculptures
of his own body

4 The Design
Museum Holon,
outside Tel
Aviv, Israel,
was designed
by Ron Arad
Architects
and opened in
March 2010

figure is him, is only him. This is everyman. The most recent work of mine is going to be the opening of the Holon Design Museum[4]. Although the Holon project was five years' work, it's still the latest work of mine because it's about to open, in a month's time.

MF Why is the show called Restless?

RA The show is called Restless, maybe, because I am restless. To jump from one project to another, it's restlessness. I am not a methodical person. Also there is a lot of movement in the show. We had the idea that every rocking chair would rock, so the show is going to be very restless. There are a couple of last year's students of mine who are good with mechanical things who are developing devices to rock the chairs, some with timers, some constantly. There's that and there are lots of big screens and I have a book that is called Restless Furniture. I like that it's restless and that furniture is something people connect with resting.

MF You were born in Israel. When did you come to London and why?

RA I grew up in a very progressive home. Both my parents are artists. When I was young, I thought me and my friends were the centre of the world, like every group of young people does. Then I found myself here in 1973. I can't remember exactly leaving Tel Aviv. I didn't pack my LPs or anything. I just found myself here and somehow, without too much planning, I found myself at the AA[5].

I went to some parties at the AA. It was fantastic. I discovered the people who played invisible tennis in Antonioni's film Blow Up were all AA students, like hardcore socialist architects. It seemed like a good place, so I joined the queue. I didn't have a portfolio. I didn't take it seriously, going to the interview. When they asked me why did I want to be an architect I told them, 'I don't. My mother wants me to be an architect.' And that was true because every time I had the pencil she said, 'Oh, that's a good drawing, be an architect,' to make sure I didn't become an artist.

They wanted to see my portfolio. I said, 'I don't have a portfolio. I have a 6B pencil. What do you want me to do?' I was cocky. I was a brat. Later, one of the people on the panel said, 'Don't do that again in an interview. We offered you a place but nearly didn't.'

So I went to the AA. Then I tried to work for an architecture practice when I graduated, but I didn't last long. It's difficult to work for other people. After lunch one day, I didn't come back. The practice was in Hampstead and I walked down the street. I went to a scrapyard behind the Roundhouse. I picked up this Rover seat and I made myself a frame and this piece sucked me into this world of design. If someone had told me a week before that I was going to be a furniture designer, I would think they were crazy, but this piece sucked me in. I dread to think what it diverted me from.

MF What happened after that?

RA I found a space in Covent Garden – before Covent Garden was given over to multinationals. It was still an exotic place. I found myself a studio without knowing what I was going to do there. I started doing some things and it was really good being in Covent Garden where a lot of cultural tourists used to come and look for excitement. There was a very influential little shop by someone called Paul Smith with concrete walls and with a different display in the window every night, and an avant-garde jewellery shop.

My first place, One Off, was in Neal Street. I actually taught myself to weld because we clad everything in steel. When we moved out, we packed everything up and it was shipped to Vitra[6]. At Neal Street was the cantilevered staircase that was, in a way, a

5 London's Architectural Association School of Architecture

6 The Vitra Design Museum in Weil am Rhein, Germany, acquired the interior of Arad's One Off studio in 1989

'You can't stay primitive for long. You get better and better technically'

keyboard of a synthesiser. As you walked down the steps, amazing music played, then you had to ask, 'Can I buy the tape that you're playing?' This was before CDs. No, you just made the music.

After that we found this place in Chalk Farm, which had been a piano workshop and a sweatshop – when we got here there were sewing machines everywhere. We made this roof that was meant to last ten years, but 20 years later it's still here and we're still here.

MF Your work straddles design, art and architecture. How do you describe yourself?

RA I am a designer, but I do other things as well. We do architecture, we do design and we do work that is outside the design world. It lives in collections in art galleries and it makes it difficult for some people to accept that there's no... [trails off]. I don't like the word 'crossover', I don't like terms like 'design-art'. It's all nonsense.

I think design is in a similar place to where photography used to be 20 to 25 years ago and people questioned the fact that a piece of art can be made using a camera and not an easel and brushes. That debate used to be interesting for a while, then it got boring, then it disappeared. Now, something that might suggest or hint at a function cannot be part of the art world. It's a very old-fashioned, conservative idea and I hope it will disappear.

There was a time when a debate was interesting between art and design and crossing over and working between disciplines. What's interesting now is what's in front of you: is it an interesting piece or is it not? I don't want to stop doing knives and forks for brands such as WMF to make it easier for curators to hold on to their job at some national institution.

Hella Jongerius
'Why make new stuff every year? I'm happy to work on the classics'

The Dutch designer invited us into her Berlin studio to discuss her work, her collaborations with a small number of brands and her move from Rotterdam to the German capital.

Marcus Fairs You're part of the great generation of Dutch designers that emerged in the 1990s. Why did you leave Rotterdam?

Hella Jongerius I graduated from Design Academy Eindhoven in 1993. I lived in Rotterdam and had a studio there for 15 years. Everything was so perfect. I had a nice house, a nice studio, a nice team, good clients. I moved to Berlin five years ago because I wanted a change. I was really fed up with being a people-manager. We wanted to move as a family. I wanted to have a small studio, to find myself again in a starter's position, because I'm good there.

MF Why Berlin?

HJ I wanted to be in Europe because, at heart, I am a European. We looked into some cities and Berlin fitted best. It's a big city but it feels like a village. It's a green city. There's not a huge design community here but I have clients all over the world, so I don't have to depend on what's going on in the city. But the main thing is that there's not a stress about money in Berlin.

MF Tell us about your studio here.

HJ I don't have a workshop any more, but now that I work with larger companies like Vitra, there are huge teams in those companies who are doing the hands-on work. These companies have highly professional teams and specialist machines. So I make small models, but I'm spoilt because the companies can do much nicer models. Also my clients have their own research and development people working for me. I can ask them, 'Can you make this model or this fabric or colour?' So it's a huge network and I'm the spider.

MF What kinds of projects are you working on?

HJ I have a very small group of clients. I really am very picky who I work with because I want to have a longer relationship with clients and really build a collection for a company. So I work on textiles for Maharam in New York; I do four or five textiles a year for the US market. And then I do furniture for Vitra, but I'm also their art director for colours, textiles and surfaces. We did new colours for all the Eames plastic chairs. And now we've started on Vitra's back catalogue of Prouvé and Eames. I find it very hard to find any energy to make new stuff. Why make new stuff every year? I don't believe we have to have more stuff, so I'm happy to work on the classics. It's less waste. We just have to lift it up to a new level.

I work for the airline KLM, so I have an aviation part in my portfolio. We did the business-class cabins for the 747. We did all

Name
Hella Jongerius
Occupation
Industrial
designer
Company
Jongeriuslab
Location
Her studio, Berlin
Date
June 2013

the soft parts but also the chairs, so it's the full interior. Now we're working on the economy cabins for the 777 and the Dreamliner planes. And I just did the interior of the UN delegates' lounge in New York with Rem Koolhaas, Irma Boom, Louise Schouwenberg and Gabriel Lester.

MF You said you don't believe we need more stuff. Can you talk about that a bit more? Isn't it the job of a designer to create new things?

HJ On one hand, we don't need more things. But also I believe a designer can use her talent to update a collection and also be sustainable. Making stuff is just one design solution. I know I can do something new in aviation because there's not a lot going on; they need me, as a designer, to produce physical stuff. But Vitra

Above
KLM's Boeing 747 business-class interior, designed by Hella Jongerius

Hella Jongerius

has great stuff. It needs me on another level and that is what I find interesting.

MF Most other designers are quite promiscuous. They work with a brand, do a product and then move on. Do you have a problem with that approach?

HJ I don't believe in working for everybody. It's a waste of energy – everything would look the same. A company has got to choose the people who can give it an identity, in the physical work, that give it a real signature, so it doesn't have to have marketing stories.

I also believe that when a company works longer with a designer, you can really trust each other. Nowadays you can't trust one another, because you never know what the other is doing. You are in competition all the time. If this competition is gone, you can really build on a collection that's not only about money but also invention. It's another way of working and it's less about ego. It's also a sustainable way of thinking for the profession, and for capitalism and consumerism.

MF You've always described yourself as an industrial designer, but a lot of your work looks very hand-crafted.

HJ I call myself an industrial designer because I believe the industry needs this crafty approach. At the start of my career I only did self-initiated projects and it was always a theme of mine to make individual products in an industrial way. To do individual pieces is just not interesting to me because that's just a hobby. As soon as a piece is in the machinery, in the system, as soon as you start talking about a market and money, you can reach a lot of people,

'If my ideas of individuality and creativity resonate with the consumer, the product is more than just slick, cheap mass production'

you can change the system. If my ideas of individuality and creativity resonate with the consumer, then the product is more than just slick, cheap mass production.

So that's why I call myself an industrial designer. I know I am not a traditional industrial designer, sending technical drawings from my computer to a company. I have questions and I like to change the way we produce. And I can only do that if I work within the system itself.

MF So you're not a designer who flies in, does some sketches, then flies out again.

HJ No. I'm part of the whole. I have been working with companies for a long time, ten to 15 years, so I have a full picture of where we're going. Then you really can make change, you know all the layers, you can take larger steps and waste less energy. A company knows exactly what it wants, so if you have the full picture, you can really guide it and have a debate together and build a collection and a company. KLM is a corporate company in a difficult industry. It's very demanding, very restricted and very commercial. The people speak a language that was new to me, and I spoke a language that was new to them. But after two years, we now really know where to go, where to steer and what the main problems are. We can make larger plans over ten years, things that really make sense and are not marketing tricks – a really slow revolution.

MF So what can you offer a commercial company like KLM?

HJ At first the project was smaller. The first question was, 'Can you do the carpet and the curtains and the seat covers?' So they knew me from an industrial, textile background. And then at a certain moment I said, 'This chair, I can do that much better. Give me the chair.' And they trusted me, so we went on. When I look back at my first PowerPoint, that was really weird. But it was for the marketing department, which means they were all young, just starting. That also helps – when there is new energy and they want to improve something. I think we were lucky. We had a chemistry together. We trusted each other. I gave them a masterclass in design, they gave me a masterclass in aviation and we did something good and we're not finished yet. We're just starting.

MF Is the ambition to make the cabin look better, or to make flying more comfortable?

HJ The main idea is to make a more tactile surrounding, more luxury, more privacy. If you travel, you know how exhausting it is. And as soon as you are on the plane, you have extra hours because you can't telephone, you can't be on the internet, you could feel like you are on holiday, you can have a bird's perspective on life, you're off the ground. It's magical. So it is an outstanding opportunity to add something tactile, human. For business class that is easy, because there is already luxury and privacy. Now I'm doing it for economy and it's quite difficult, because the restrictions are very narrow and it's more inconvenient. But as I said, I am aware I can only take little steps.

Neri&Hu
'Architects in the US may be lost, but they have no projects. In China we're lost and we're building cities'

Names
Rossana Hu
and Lyndon Neri
Occupation
Architects
Company
Neri&Hu
Location
Design
Republic
Commune,
Shanghai
Date
November 2012

Rossana Hu and Lyndon Neri invited us to the opening of their Design Republic Commune gallery and store in Shanghai, where they discussed the need for a design manifesto in their country.

Marcus Fairs You're both architects but you also run a gallery and shop. What is Design Republic?

Rossana Hu After we started our architecture practice here in Shanghai we started Design Republic, which is really a platform for design. We began with a retail concept, but there are other things we wanted to incorporate into the retail environment. One of them was education: educating the public about design, to bring designers from different parts of the world to China, to speak, to show their work, to engage in a dialogue with the designers here.

Lyndon Neri The idea is to bring the best of what the world can offer to China. And hopefully, one day, our aspiration is to bring the best of what China can offer, from a design point of view, to the world.

RH This week we are opening the Design Republic Commune space to the public and having a two-day symposium called Manifesto. We've invited guest speakers from all over the world to come and talk about design in different ways. If we don't do this, and we only show and sell products, it's just meaningless.

And vice versa. If we only do the talks and you read about these products but you don't see them, you don't touch them, that's also meaningless. And that was the case in Shanghai before Design Republic opened. You couldn't see classic modern design anywhere. There were no design museums, there were no shops that sell modern classics. People were just not interested.

MF Where did this idea of manifestos come from?

LN It started about seven years ago, when Rossana and I edited a book called Persistence of Vision: Shanghai Architects in Dialogue. We interviewed 50 architects practising in Shanghai. We asked them 12 questions. At the back of our mind was the notion of trying to find a manifesto in a city that is so busy, a city that is just building like mad. We realised it was important to make sure that people are thinking, having a discourse.

RH It all derived from when we first started working here. We were talking about the conditions of working here with both local and overseas Chinese who had returned. And everyone is so busy and has no time to think, no time to talk to one another. And every time you do have time to talk, it's five to ten minutes, and

you can never really engage in a meaningful way. And we thought, 'Okay, if everyone feels that way, that means everyone must welcome the chance to engage.'

We did the book as an effort to bring about community. And it did, I think. It made all the people we interviewed rethink why it is that they're here. We asked about culture, space, location, work, the responsibility of architects and designers, whether they're happy with what they're doing here, those types of questions.

We wanted Design Republic to be a platform and the retail part just became the easiest thing to start, because the form of a shop is something that people can understand: you sell products. But there are other things we wanted to do. We wanted to create a brand that incorporates other designers in China, to bring about a Chinese voice in modern design; to engage in the problems that exist here today.

MF How does that relate to what you're doing here? A lot of the speakers at your Manifesto talks are from the West.

RH From the book project we realised a lot of people were asking what today's manifesto in design is. And actually that's not just a Chinese problem – it's a global problem. Architects feel lost. We're no longer confined within 'big A' architecture the way I thought we were 15 or 20 years ago. It was probably easier to design then because everyone shared certain beliefs. We believe in manifestos, we believe that you need to stake your belief. If you know your dream, then you can chase after it.

LN And be rigorous about it.

RH And also we notice the absence of a collective voice. The absence of a modern Chinese architecture and design language.

LN In China, the phenomenon of copying is great. So people look at magazines and go, 'I could sort of do this minimalist thing. I'll

'Architects feel lost. And it's not just a Chinese problem – it's a global problem'

have the contractor do something like this.' It's done in such a 'mama huhu' way: such a half-arsed, half-baked way that it becomes, you know, scary.

MF Shanghai is quite funny that way, because you have these Western-style skyscrapers with Chinese details bolted to the top. It's surreal.

RH I remember having a discussion with my teacher at Princeton. I remember talking to him about my thesis proposal, discussing the problem of Modernism, and regionalism versus globalism. He thought that to modernise means basically what Rem Koolhaas believes: the tabula rasa. There's no history. That's all baggage you don't need. But I still insist that you are who you are. None of us can erase our past. You bring the baggage with you and you've got to work with the baggage you have.

So how do you then exist as a contemporary architect, working with a modern architectural language? How do you exist in this environment, what is it that we take with us? Maybe it's not our history from the Ming and Qing dynasties, or even earlier. Maybe it's what we see today. Maybe it's that's across your longtang[1] window, that you can see in your neighbour's bathroom, or it's the broom that everyone hangs up. Maybe it's those very mundane, everyday things that give you a clue as to what to design.

But also we recognise that we're only one part of the world, and we're only one very small part of the larger Chinese-modern context. I like to learn from other disciplines, to learn from, say, Chinese modern literature, Chinese modern art, Chinese modern music, and how they have evolved to where they are today.

The modern Chinese language, the writing system, is actually influenced by English writing. The same with poetry. People have gone abroad, studied and brought things back. You know, if you look at the Chinese architects who are doing significant work here, almost all of them have done work abroad: Yung Ho Chang, Ma Qingyun, Ma Yansong. Most of us went abroad, but now we are all back here, taking what we've learned and creating something new.

LN Omer Arbel[2] said something very interesting today when he was asked what he would say to Chinese architecture students. He said that growing up, it was easy to model his career on the protagonists of his time. In his case it was Rem Koolhaas. But then quickly he realised it was not just unattainable, it was so abstract that it was meaningless to people in Vancouver. So he started finding meaning within the context that he was practising, and that became interesting.

MF You mentioned that these are global issues. To what extent are they issues in China, too?

RH It is even more of an issue here because more people are working here, and it's at a faster pace.

LN It's amplified, exaggerated.

RH So if you get lost, you get lost faster. And if you fall, you fall deeper.

LN A lot of architects in the US are lost, but there are no projects. So they could be lost and not build. Here, we are lost and we are building cities. We're building cities, for crying out loud!

RH If you tell people this kind of stuff here, they don't understand why you're even doing it. They don't understand the need to have a manifesto. In the West, when you tell people about this, at least they understand why you're searching. They may not have it, they might be lost, but they know that they are lost. Here, people are lost without knowing they're lost. That's a real danger.

MF So the manifesto needs to be figured out pretty soon. How are you going to do that?

RH I don't really see that there needs to be an end. I don't think it's like saying, 'Okay, once we formulate our manifesto, then this is it.'

MF You produced a little Manifesto booklet for the opening event.

RH We really worked hard on that. We really thought about it. And the reason why it's mostly blank pages is so you can write your own down. They're offset with quotes from Chinese writers and poets and Western writers' quotes about life, about ideals, about utopias. This helps you set the tone. It's the beginning, but the key is that you're searching for something, and that your work will, hopefully, stand for something.

Yves Béhar

'Designing hardware and software at the same time is a new frontier in design'

The Swiss-born designer spoke with us about moving to California to work with technology companies and the way their attitude to design has changed since the 1990s.

Marcus Fairs Do you ever think what would have happened if you hadn't left Europe? How did the environment on the West Coast influence the kind of designer you've become?

Name
Yves Béhar
Occupation
Industrial
designer
Company
Fuseproject
Location
100% Design,
London
Date
September 2012

Yves Béhar It's hard to tell. I think what moving to California has done is put me, first of all, in front of a whole new field that needed design. Technology was not 'designed' in the early 1990s. Computers were not in your home. Devices were not in your pocket or on your wrist. A whole new field of design has emerged out of that and I could anticipate that was needed. What I should also say is that I'm an economic refugee from Switzerland. Because, to be very honest, there wasn't the kind of industry in Switzerland that could support the kind of experimentation and view that companies were taking over in California. If I had stayed, I would probably be a very small studio, maybe me and a couple of interns, versus having large-scale operations that allow me to do all these different things.

MF In the early days, what kind of companies did you get involved with that you couldn't have been involved with in Europe?

YB In the first studio I started at, 20 years ago, they were working on mostly exhibit design and furniture design. They were working with Herman Miller, which back then was a discovery. All the work that had been done by Charles Eames and George Nelson in the 1950s and '60s had been almost forgotten by the early '90s because their work wasn't widely distributed then. So, in a sense, I discovered furniture design.

I worked with consultants like Frog Design and Lunar Design, and with companies like Apple, Hewlett Packard and Silicon Graphics. That was in the early days when people were thinking about the desktop computer going from being an object in the back room of a workplace to being an object that's living with you, that you can carry around. The first year I joined Lunar, I think, the first laptop was being developed for Apple, so there was this whole new portable field.

MF What was the attitude of those computer companies towards design? Did they get it?

YB Some got it. The majority didn't get it. It's honestly not that different from the way that large industry in Europe doesn't get it. I'm not talking about furniture and home accessories companies – they are tiny relative to large European industry. I mean, it's not that different from the way large industry in Europe uses design today, as something to add on at the end. The only company that got it back then was Steve Jobs and Apple. At the time, they were using many different design firms – mostly Frog Design, which was Steve Jobs' partner in the early days.

Most of the time I would go to companies and I would be surrounded by business people. They would look at me and say, 'What's the return on investment for design?' They really did not understand what we were doing there. It was not a factor in determining a company's success, why you would do things or how you would approach a user. So I had to battle through these years of having to prove to people that design actually creates a lot of value. Obviously we got a lot from Apple, which has, for the past ten years, done so well. Now design is a model. Design is at the forefront, design is on the board of companies, design is part of truly building businesses.

MF That conversation is getting easier then, is it?

YB Absolutely. It's funny now because I have a lot of clients from Europe. They're trying to look at the way Apple works and trying to put designers back in a leadership position rather than a following position. And that means a huge change for designers.

MF Apple has recently accused its rivals of copying its hardware and software. How hard is it to innovate, to push the boundaries of design forward?

YB It's hard and it demands full commitment from a business. The investments are immense, the investments in the underlying technologies, in doing something a little different. But I think people are getting it now. The leadership Apple has taken, of course, makes a lot of companies want to emulate it.

But what I'm saying is kind of ridiculous because when we think about good design in the field of technology, we look at Apple and we think that's the only way. We think Apple is the only way to have good design and good technology married together. And what I often think is that there are five or six different ways to do what Apple is doing. So when business people come to us and say, 'We want to be like Apple,' I always say, 'No. You have to find your own direction. You have to find your own vision of who you want to be.'

MF Is part of your role as a designer to help them find that vision?

YB Absolutely. And there are ways. We built Jawbone[1] as a brand. It was a startup that had never created a product. The notion that design is this one silver monolith, the Apple way, we challenged that with materials and textures that are varied and much more sensory. This whole notion of bent metal as a process, we invented that at Jawbone. So Jawbone is one example of how technology can be integrated into products in a different way. It's not about being better or being like something else but about building your own reference points, building your own technologies, your own way of making things and your own way of connecting with the consumer.

MF What is your relationship with Jawbone? You're not just a freelance designer it hires when it's got a product launch. You're involved in the corporate structure.

YB I've been working with Jawbone for ten years in a partnership model, which means I'm one of the executives in the company who is part of every decision taken. I'm at the same level as the chief financial officer or the chief technology officer and that allows me to understand everything that's going on in the company. We invest in things when we can and we create new lines of business where we can find more opportunities. My role is essentially to be the chief curator of a growing business, from making essential products to stretching them into new dimensions of customisation.

For example, we have a customisation engine that allows people to decide what colours and textures they want to combine on the Jambox[2], which became the number one-selling speaker in America, in all the Apple Stores. We are also stretching the

'We challenged the notion that design is this one silver monolith, the Apple way'

brand in cultural places, having it be a mainstream product and at the same time a product that can be in a gallery setting.

My role is to stretch the company into new areas where design can play around and where the brand can be presented in the right way. What we're still working on is this wearability, the idea that technology is becoming wearable, that it's giving you important data about how you live, your sleep cycles, your movements. So this device on my wirst allows you to keep track of how much you move, how much you sleep.

MF What is it? What does it do?

YB This is the Up bracelet. It's a device that allows you to track your activity and track your sleep. You can even see the difference between your light sleep and your deep sleep. You can keep track of your friends and loved ones – or, as we like to call them, your team. Like a sports team. You can tell them to do more and get off the couch or you can encourage them if they're running or doing any physical activity.

MF This is one of the key areas in which design is changing in the twenty-first century. In the twentieth century, technology was in its own box. It was the computer. But you're talking about technology embedded in your life, that monitors what's happening in your life. What are your views on that?

YB We think the notion that computers or your internet experience happen only on a screen or in a box is going away. When we call the internet a 'thing' – which is the data and the knowledge and the search and experiences that we have – it becomes a thing we wear, a thing we put on our head, on our body, in our shoes.

For me, what's interesting is, rather than asking technology to do something for you, pressing a button or looking for something on a phone, I think technology is becoming more and more embedded in our lives. So we're anticipating those wants and those needs and responding to them in a way that is going to be a lot more seamless.

MF Are you working with any companies on this that you can tell us about?

YB I am working with companies on this that I can't tell you about.

MF Then can you elaborate on this a bit more? Technology is escaping from the computer and attaching itself to our clothes and our furniture. How else is technology changing the world? And how are you, as a designer, helping to embed these technologies?

YB We've built a user-experience space in the studio. What we're excited about with digital products – the products we touch with our fingers right now, surfaces such as a phone screen – is how designing these products is so similar to designing physical products. When you think about the identity of something, the way it looks, the texture, the functionality, where to touch it, the ten-foot view, the iconography viewed from ten feet: all those notions are exactly the same whether you're designing hardware or software, whether you're doing a physical button or organising the functionality of an app. What I'm really interested in is that when these things are designed together as one, new paradigms and experiences are happening.

Let me just say one thing here and maybe it'll be a little provocative. Nobody is really doing that today. Apple is designing its product and its software separately. The skeuomorphism that you find in the user interface on Apple products, the faux leather on the calendar, that's not on the hardware products.

So designing these two things at the same time is completely new, a really fascinating exercise as a designer. It's the same as when you design a piece of furniture: you think of the foam that's inside, how it's going to respond to the body, the way it looks on the outside. Then think about the fact that technology is usually designed completely separately – it's as if somebody was designing the way this chair feels when I sit in it and somebody else was designing the outer look of it. That's a whole new blue ocean for us as designers. It's a new frontier.

MF Let's rewind a bit. You mentioned this term 'skeuomorphism'. In Apple devices people particularly go on about it. You have this sophisticated glass and aluminium phone and then the diary's got a leather grain on it and the bookshelf is made to look like wood. Is that a design failure? My understanding is Apple uses those icons because your brain is configured to expect a physical diary, so it puts you in a 'diary' frame of mind.

YB You could use that exact explanation for a hardware product. You could say, 'Well I don't know what a tablet is. I don't know how to use it. Let's make it look like my leather-bound notebook.' Obviously they didn't go there with hardware, so why did they go there with the software? It's a really good question. There are now many good companies looking at it in a way that's quite interesting. Apple is actually a little bit behind in that area.

MF What is the way forward, then? You said you reject the notion of making a smartphone diary look like a leather-bound diary, so what should it look like? What is the approach that leads to the response to that question?

YB The approach I'm looking at is to design both these products at the same time. Design the interface and the hardware at the same time so you really think about, for example, the mood, the appropriate colour, the appropriate function for the calendar. What are the emotions that go with it? Do I feel stressed or challenged by the complexity of a calendar? Do I need to divide it into, for example, hours? Or is my first view about knowing what's happening in the morning and the afternoon? As I zoom in, can I see more detail? There are 15 different things I'm supposed to do in a day, but if I know what I'm doing in the morning, that's okay. I can see it in broad strokes. There's a way to look at a calendar that's not imagining it as paper.

MF So by using the physical object as a reference point, designers are failing to exploit the potential of digital interfaces?

YB The opportunities are there and the fact that we're not taking these opportunities as designers, I think, is lazy.

MF Can you give an example of something that does this job really well?

YB We're about to launch the tablet version of the $100 laptop and we're working on a general interface. How do children navigate 1000 applications, each with a different learning tool? How should we organise these tools? For example, a child might say, 'I want to be an astronaut,' or 'I want to be a mathematician.'

So we could use that as an entry point for arranging the apps around, say, math.

MF What is the $100 laptop?

YB It's a project I've been working on for the American non-profit organisation One Laptop Per Child. I've been working on the design of the $100 laptop for about seven years. In 2007 we launched the first version. There have been four upgrades since then. We have put three million laptops in the hands of children. In Peru there are a million in the hands of children and in Uruguay every child between six and 18 has one. We have developments in 30 or 40 countries. The next version is a tablet we've been working on for a while. We'll be making some announcements in a few months regarding that.

Above
Big Jambox
wireless speaker
designed by
Yves Béhar
for Jawbone

Yves Béhar

MF So the $100 laptop was a project to make computers accessible to people who wouldn't normally be able to afford a laptop?

YB Exactly. To the developing world. I mean, if you think about any country outside the Western countries we would normally deal with, we usually think about Uruguay or Peru or Ethiopia. The challenge is, how do you digitise those populations if university students, when they're 25 years old, have missed out on all the technical learning that happens when you're six, seven, eight, nine years old, when you're learning how to code, learning how to explore? This is a way to digitise, to teach all those skills to an entire population at a very affordable cost.

MF You've become associated with the notion of sustainable design and I guess this is a sort of social sustainability—providing opportunities to people who might not otherwise have them. What is your vision of sustainable design and what does it mean?

YB Sustainability is a progression. If you look at all our manufacturing facilities and all our industrial sites, those are the places that have to be retooled and rethought. There is no doubt in my mind

'Designers need to be embedded in efforts to retool industry because we need to help industry move in the right places'

that this work will be happening. So while industry is thinking about retooling itself to be more efficient, to respond to consumer demands and to use less energy, there is a huge opportunity for designers to participate. Because when you're thinking about how to better produce goods and reuse materials, design is a big part of that. My sense is that we need to be very much embedded in efforts of retooling industry because we need to help industry move in those right places, in ways where better design will come out of the shift.

MF What is the definition of sustainability, then? Is it using fewer resources, is it having fewer things in the world? Because there is a paradox between designers talking about sustainability and the role of the designer to bring new objects into being.

YB Well, the most interesting place to be in life, I think, is at the centre of a paradox. And design represents that kind of paradox.

For example, design is regarded as a luxurious practice. It is often celebrated for a level of refinement that makes things extremely expensive. So design is, in a way, often disconnected from its intent, which is to reach a majority. That's an interesting paradox.

I personally believe that attainability is extremely important and the more we can create high-quality and sustainable products that are attainable for the largest number, the more we are advancing the idea that sustainability is the way forward for business, and for people in general. My definition of good design is design that helps move forward the ideas of the twenty-first century. For me, that's what good design does. It accelerates the adoption of these good ideas, and our role as designers is to do exactly that.

MF Can you give an example of how you have put that definition of good design into practice?

YB It took us about three years to retool the Puma factories around the world, because they make about 80 million pairs of shoes. We were able to reduce the amount of energy used in making shoeboxes by 65 percent and eliminate all printing chemicals from the process. The box is a flimsy recycled-cardboard piece that is held in place by a recycled PTE material. The combination of these creates the structure needed for shoes to travel on boats, conveyor belts and so on. What happens in the stores has been fascinating. We've been able to get rid of most of the vinyl plastic bags, because our new cloth Clever Little Bag gets used after the purchase to take the shoes home.

This is one of those projects where initially it's not very glamorous. Every designer wants to design the next super-cool collection of shoes for Puma or Nike, right? But those are temporary projects, the projects that are going to get a lot of press, that are going to get you some fun launches. They'll last, what, two, three seasons, maybe a year? Then that will be gone. I actually got really excited about this project because if we're able to retool the company to make 80 million shoeboxes that are going to ship all these shoes, that's a first step toward something that will have longevity.

MF How does a project like that come about? Did Puma approach you and say, 'We want you to design a cool trainer and we'll throw lots of cool parties,' and you said, 'No, let's actually look a bit deeper'?

YB We've done projects with Puma before and we've been having that dialogue. The previous CEO at Puma, who had been there for 15 years, was extremely interested in sustainability and deeply committed to creating a social-engagement platform for the company. This became the project by which all that strategy was revealed. They came to me with a question, and I think those are the best projects, because most projects come with a brief and

Yves Béhar

1 Jawbone is a
consumer
technology
company based
in San Francisco,
California

2 Jambox
is a wireless
Bluetooth speaker
developed
by Jawbone

most answers come contained in the brief. But this time they simply said, 'We don't know whether we can make this shoebox better. Can we?'

The shoebox they had been using previously was this big red box with a lot of bright colours and you could see it from afar – it was the best branded shoebox out there. They took their most successful piece of signage and asked, 'Can you do something else with it?' – with the hope that maybe there was a possibility to do something better with no specific expectation. I think that's why it turned out so well, because we threw the ball really far away when it came to the design, worked really hard for three years with German logistics engineers. If you think about it, those few words changed an entire ecosystem of manufacturing.

MF You seem to have very sustainable relationships with the companies you work for. Do you think the design world thinks too short term?

YB Here's what I'm interested in. I'm interested in doing the best possible work. That's all that is interesting to me. If I think about how I work with clients over a long period of time, things get better, they understand me better, they're able to embed important notions for us over a period of time, I understand their market and their goals over three, four or five years.

With Jawbone, I was thinking 'Jawbone' every day for ten years. I'm the most senior person on the Jawbone team who's been there the longest, outside of the founder. With Herman Miller it's the same. I've been working with them for 11 years and we don't have to brief each other so much. I may come to Herman Miller or Jawbone with an idea, they might come to me with an idea. We agree to explore that idea together rather than having a strict brief and deadline. In those long-term relationships, that's when the best design work happens. If I didn't have this relationship with Jawbone, there's no way we would have worked for three and a half years to launch the Up bracelet. People get tired and move away and go to the next thing.

MF If a brand approached you and said, 'Hey, we love your work. We just need you to do something that will get us loads of press attention,' would you walk away from it?

YB I think if press attention is the goal, if the goal is to tell a new story about what a company believes about its sustainability or social platform, then there's nothing wrong with press attention. If a company is collecting ten designers just for their names, to make a splash somewhere, and it's not part of a long-term change within the company or a new story that it's trying to tell, I think that's a waste of time.

There is nothing wrong with designers admitting that we are an important component – and sometimes *the* most important component – of a story being told in the right way. Companies are finally starting to realise that the designer's work is what customers are experiencing first hand. It's not the advertising, it's not the marketing. How people are talking about a product is how they look at it, feel it, use it and take it into their homes. We are in a completely new place compared to the advertising-driven world we lived in throughout the '80s and '90s. We're in a world where

'Companies are finally starting to realise that the designer's work is what people experience first hand'

people are doing their own reviews, where people communicate directly with companies, where anybody can market a product simply by endorsing it and liking it in the social sphere.

MF Last week you sent me a little statement you'd written, and it started off, 'Design is generous, advertising is not generous, marketing is not generous.' What do you mean by that?

YB I mean that what gets me and all my designer friends up in the morning is the ability to create something that will have meaning in somebody's life. And what gets us up in the morning is creating a new experience, creating something that is significant. It isn't to sell something that's already there. It's really to create. And when you create, you're giving. To me, that's the most important thing about the profession of design: it's a giving profession. You're trying to give something, to make something that many more people will experience – not just you.

Ilse Crawford

'The interior is the life of the building, but so often it's just seen as a shopping list'

Interior designer Ilse Crawford was chair of the jury at the INSIDE Festival, held in Barcelona in 2011. To set the scene, we spoke to her about her design philosophy and the influence of her Scandinavian background on her work.

Marcus Fairs Tell us about yourself.

Ilse Crawford As the head of Studioilse, I mostly design interiors. But, in fact, we do a lot more than that here. Because, I think, interiors are ultimately where we live, they are a lot more than pieces of furniture. They're really about interior life, how we live as human beings.

MF How do you describe your work and the philosophy behind it?

IC We do a huge range of projects: residential, retail, offices and hospitality development. We've been working with developers recently to determine how to put the human being at the beginning of the programme of development, rather than the estate agent – how to make some of their buildings more liveable.

The studio essentially focuses on space from the point of view of the human being inside it. We're physical beings and ultimately buildings are a frame for life. That's how we approach them. It's not an intellectual activity. You experience interiors through your body.

MF Why isn't interior design taken as seriously as architecture?

IC Interiors are so often understood as chucking a few bits of furniture into architecture. I come at them from the other perspective completely, probably because of my Scandinavian roots. If you look at the way designers approach buildings, I would say that the majority do it from a conceptual perspective. But the Scandinavians start from the point of view of where the door will be, how you experience the space. So you have a completely different way of looking at the same conundrum. Interior design essentially joins those two things together. The interior, I think, is essentially the life of the building. But so often it's just seen as a shopping list.

MF Where is your family from?

IC My mother was Danish – from the Faroe Islands, so that's as Scandi as you can get. And my dad was Canadian. So you could say my upbringing was rather puritanical.

MF Have your Scandinavian roots influenced your work?

IC Not consciously but invariably. I was brought up, I realise now, in that Danish ideal of the warm, modern home. The Scandinavians

Name
Ilse Crawford
Occupation
Interior designer
Company
Studioilse
Location
Her studio,
London
Date
June 2011

very early on approached modern furniture from the point of view of using natural materials and wood instead of metal. Scandinavians, particularly Alvar Aalto, disapproved of what they called the inhuman touch of cold steel. So, yes, I was certainly brought up with that feeling. Also, the thing about Scandinavia is that it kind of became modern on a national scale much earlier than, for example, Britain. So I grew up thinking that everyone was modern. There's still a big gap, I would say, between Sweden and Denmark and Britain.

In Swedish you say *besjala* to put soul into a place. In Danish you talk about a place like it is an embrace. I think you can do that, for example, in an office. It's not about having sweet sofas everywhere. It's about looking at the things you do every day

Ilse Crawford

and making them work on a human scale, like having a great kitchen, making the photocopy room fantastic, the possibility of, say, having movable shelving around you where you can put your objects and still have a sense of being connected to others. It's working out if you like the politics, the organisation of how you have conversations. It's having a common room rather than lots of conference rooms, which are ultimately rather confrontational.

Obviously you have to balance that with practical needs, but I think, historically, the tectonic, practical and functional have ended up driving the wagon, and ultimately you've got things the wrong way around. The design should be driven by life and the practical stuff should be the stuff that makes that happen, not the other way around.

MF Can you provide some examples of how you apply your approach?

IC We put wellbeing at the core of all our projects, and when we talk about wellbeing, we certainly don't mean simply a spa. For example, we did a small residential development in Hong Kong called TwoTwoSix Hollywood Road that was about making a connection to its location, so it didn't create a sort of black hole in the street, which is common in most developments there;

'We put wellbeing at the core of all our projects, and when we talk about wellbeing, we don't mean simply a spa'

the buildings are very introverted and you lose any sense of them being inhabited. Then, within the apartments, we started from the point of view of life. We gave them a strong material language, making sure there was the right combination of warm and cool materials, because we all want to have a tactile connection to where we live, right down to the finishes. We made sure the windows were fully openable. We had places where you could put things easily and practical stuff like lots of storage. That's also part of being human.

Another project we've done is Mathias Dahlgren's restaurant at the Grand Hôtel in Stockholm. I think it was one of our most effective projects. The starting point was good because Mathias really believed in the power of interiors and trusted us to interpret his philosophy of food in three dimensions. Because while he might be making the most amazing food, for people to fully understand it they need to feel it on all the other levels, to experience it. So it could be smelled, heard and felt.

It was two restaurants: a fine-dining restaurant for slow food and a food bar, which is a more everyday experience of the same food. It was fascinating having to do two expressions of the same man's food. One is about a long, drawn-out, sensual experience, and we put that behind a secret door, the opposite of what you might normally do to make it a special place. Then the food bar we made more robust in its materials, with encaustic tiles and wood. You can sit together; it's more masculine, you might say, but very much an expression of the ingredients and the way of cooking. And that's something that I think is interesting with interiors: you can take what's going on in one sense and translate it through to the other senses.

We had discussions around a few sixteenth-century block-board tables that we wanted to include. They were a touch wobbly and Mathias was quite worried about that, because of course chefs are quite worried about everything being perfect. We just said, 'Let's try it for a month. We'll give you a few words to say when people sit down at this table: "Look, this table has been around for 400 years and thousands of meals have been eaten on this table, and that's a connection to Mathias and the roots of his food."' After that, everybody wanted those tables.

So I think the power of an interior to amplify and express the life of a place, the content, the brand is huge and so often underestimated – especially in very commercial, corporate situations. Of course it's understandable: you have quantity surveyors, you have project managers and so on who need to get things in on time and on budget. But what you end up with is a world with no identity that's absolutely uninhabitable.

Ben Terrett

'Web design is only just getting started. There's a lot to do – particularly with interface'

Ben Terrett is a designer who went to work for the UK government. We spoke to him about his pioneering approach to public-sector web design and his gov.uk website, which was named Design of the Year 2013 by London's Design Museum.

Marcus Fairs In your Design Indaba talk you spoke about digital space being a new paradigm. What did you mean by that?

Ben Terrett I think it goes back to when I started the job. There's this huge task and you're just looking around for inspiration and where to begin. I think it takes, like, five, ten minutes, and you start looking at British design and British history and you realise there is this huge catalogue, this canon, that goes right back to Bazalgette[1], this fantastic public-sector design. They're not just design, though they've got design elements in them. They're fantastic projects, like the sewers or the London Tube map or, like, Calvert and Kinneir's road signs[2]. We've got this great heritage of public sector design work, which is fantastic.

It became obvious to me that there were more of those examples, and the more I thought about it, the more it appeared they were trying to do a very similar thing to what we're doing. I think if you're a graphic designer working today, the future is digital. I'm part of a thing called Newspaper Club, so I love print as much as anyone else, but the future is digital. If you're a young graphic designer working today, that's where it's all at. This is a big, exciting digital project and there's this amazing heritage. If we could merge these two together, this could be absolutely amazing. That was, sort of, day one.

MF What is gov.uk?

BT We are developing gov.uk, a single-domain government website, which comes out of Martha Lane Fox's report[3]. The government asked her to look at and write about all its digital stuff and it was one of her recommendations that we have a single portal for government services. There were thousands of government websites and we closed those and we're folding them into gov.uk to make just one. The reason to do that, really, is to ensure the user doesn't have to understand government to find something out. They just go to one place and it's there. They don't have to know which government department has that information or which site has that information; they don't have to learn new things. It's not like the BBC news website, which you might go on once a day. People only go to government websites once or twice a

Name
Ben Terrett
Occupation
Designer
Company
Government
Digital Service
Location
Design Indaba,
Cape Town
Date
March 2013

year to find out a particular thing or transact with a particular service. So people shouldn't have to learn how to use that. It should be the same as booking a driving test. If we have a single domain, we can do that. This is the core of our work – not just designing but focusing on user need. The user need is really clear and simple: there's one place and one website.

MF How far do you think we have yet to go with interface design on the internet?

BT In terms of web design, user interface and the maturity of web design, I think it's only just getting started. I think there is lots to do, particularly with interface, as technology changes. You saw Alexander Chen[4] talking about Google Glass earlier, and it's really interesting, his point about there being no user interface. On Google Glass there's no button. You're just talking to it and then stuff is appearing. I think that's really fascinating.

Something we're trying to do on our site is letting design get out of the way and letting the users get to what they want. You shouldn't get to a website and say, 'Wow, look at the graphic design!' You should come to the website to find out what the

'I think if you're a graphic designer working today, the future is digital'

minimum wage is, and then go out. We haven't achieved that yet with web interface design; it's still getting in the way. There are still loads of websites where you can see the graphic design everywhere and we need to get past that. Technology will change, like Google Glass and other things we don't yet know about, and that will prompt people to work harder on interface design. But there's a long way to go. It's a really fascinating, exciting challenge.

MF Do you think designers are the best people to ask to get design out of the way?

BT I think good designers are the right people to do this stuff. If you showed the Tube map to someone in the street, they wouldn't say, 'That's design.' The design has become invisible because it's so good. It's the same with the road signs. They're a graphic-design project and they're in the Design Museum, but they weren't when they were launched and people didn't think of them as design. Good designers are absolutely the right people to do this.

MF In your talk you mentioned a little hand-drawn paper sign on the window in your office. What's that?

BT Early on, we wrote a set of design principles for the project that guide us. Number one is: start with user needs, not government

Ben Terrett

1 Joseph
Bazalgette was
the engineer
of London's
sewer network

2 Margaret
Calvert and Jock
Kinneir designed
the road and
motorway sign
system across
Britain in the
1950s and '60s

3 Martha Lane
Fox, UK 'digital
champion' from
2010 to 2013,
called for a major
overhaul of the
government's
internet services
in a 2010 report

4 Alexander Chen,
the creative
director of
Google Creative
Lab, also spoke
at Design Indaba
2013

needs. We have a relentless focus on user needs and designing for that and not letting other things get in the way.

Here's how we've visualised that in the office – it's become almost a meme. We were in a meeting once and people started talking about user need and user personas. Someone sketched a typical user on a piece of paper and I said, 'That's not right.' If this was a commercial site, you would have a particular set of users to focus on. But we're designing our site for everyone in the country, of all different ages and different literacy and web literacy. It's for everyone. I picked up the piece of paper, a big piece of flip-chart paper, and ripped a hole in it, like a square window, and stuck that on the window of the meeting room. So it says 'users' and there's an arrow pointing to this big hole, and through this hole you can look down into the street and see the users. We didn't think anything of it, but it stayed in the meeting room and no one took it down. Whenever anyone comes to the office, that's the thing they take a picture of, that's the thing they Instagram. It's a good way of visualising users, I guess.

A few weeks ago I had coffee with a guy who used to work for Henri Kay Henrion, a famous designer born in Germany. He emigrated to Britain and did lots of postwar posters for the government, posters for the post office, lots of government design work in the 1930s and '40s. This guy who used to work there said, 'Henrion always used to say that civil servants should be forced to sit looking out the window to remind them they are working for the people of the country.' And that stuck with me.

MF What sort of impact is gov.uk having on the digital strategies of other countries?

BT GDS[5] has been going less than two years, so it's really only starting, this project. Other governments from around the world, city governments and country governments, come and visit us. There's a map I used in my Design Indaba presentation, which is every government that has visited us or is planning to come and see us, and I don't know how many it is, but it's a lot. I think that's happening because we've got a very open culture, so we blog lots about what we're doing. All our code is open source – you can take the code and the design patterns and the things we've done and make your own versions from that. As a group of people, we believe in open source. That's how the best things on the web are made and we want to be part of that. I think that culture leads to people hearing about it.

MF What can other governments learn from gov.uk? How is it different from what came before?

BT If you look at the design of gov.uk, it's very simple. That comes from two things – again, from focusing on the user need and doing early user testing, and from removing things that users either told us, or that was clear from their behaviour they just didn't need. They just want the information on the page, removing everything that gets in the way of that.

The second thing is, we realised we were doing information design. We weren't just pushing pixels around a screen. I think there's a tendency, these days, for web designers to push pixels around and say, 'That looks nice,' but we've got to forget that and remember that people want information from the site, so we design something for that information. That leads you to strip away all the bits that get in the way of that information and that gives you a natural, simple look and feel, almost a Modernist simplicity. It tests fantastically well and the user feedback we get is great. People can get the information they want, quickly.

The other thing is that we're starting to be recognised in other areas. We've just been nominated for Design of the Year[6] and we didn't think anything like that would ever happen. We were just making this website for users, really. But to be nominated for something like that, alongside Renzo Piano's Shard and Thomas Heatherwick's Olympic cauldron and stuff like that, that's just been fantastic.

5 Government Digital Service, or GDS, is the unit leading the UK government's transformation to digital

6 In 2013 gov.uk was declared Design of the Year by London's Design Museum

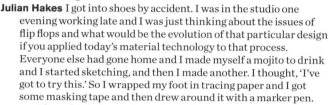

Julian Hakes

'I designed the shoe how I would design a bridge. It's a bridge for the foot'

The architect-turned-shoe designer spoke to us about his radical footwear without a footplate, which went viral after it was first featured in Dezeen in 2009.

Ben Hobson How did you make the transition from an architect to a shoe designer?

Julian Hakes I got into shoes by accident. I was in the studio one evening working late and I was just thinking about the issues of flip flops and what would be the evolution of that particular design if you applied today's material technology to that process. Everyone else had gone home and I made myself a mojito to drink and I started sketching, and then I made another. I thought, 'I've got to try this.' So I wrapped my foot in tracing paper and I got some masking tape and then drew around it with a marker pen.

If you think about a footprint in the sand, the heel and the ball are the two parts of the foot that are primarily carrying a load and need protecting. There's a little bit of transfer on the outside of the arch but not that much. So I then made this sketch with the heel and the ball protected, cut it off and just left it and thought, 'Well, that's something quite interesting.'

The next day I came back to the studio and thought, with a slightly fresher head, that this could actually work. This could actually be pushed further. I sketched it and started to draw a heel on it as well and elevate the shoe. Then we all started to play with lots of different materials in the studio and we kind of left it for a while, didn't do very much.

BH And this was back when?

JH The first ideas we had for the shoes were probably back in 2006. Back then we were very busy. We had a lot of work going on in the studio. Then round about the end of 2007, our projects in the office started to go on hold as a result of the credit crunch. So there was more time to think about other things within the studio. Our projects on bridges sometimes take up to ten years. There's a long lead time. And while we won commissions, we knew they were far off. We thought, 'Let's see what else we can explore in design.'

BH What's unique about the shoe?

JH The shoe is a single bit of material that wraps from underneath the ball of the foot to over the top and under the heel. It has no footplate in the middle, because your foot spans the gap between the heel and the front of the foot.

Name
Julian Hakes
Occupation
Architect
Location
Dezeen Space
pop-up gallery,
London
Date
September 2011

BH How did you develop it?

JH We had a foot model come in and we cast her foot in plaster and made a plaster cast. We scanned her foot over at the Royal College of Art and then started to produce this design, which was just this paper mock-up in more detail.

Then we digitised it and produced our first 3D print from this thing. At the same time we thought, 'Let's do a graphic of this 3D print,' and we sent it to Marcus Fairs at Dezeen. And that's where it really started, because later on that evening I got a call and thought it was going to be about lots of bridges and stuff, but it was none of that. There was not a single mention of any bridge or building that I'd worked on. It was all shoes. The story had passed from Dezeen to this website in America called Gizmodo

Above
The Mojito shoe designed by Julian Hakes

and it had gone right around the world and our inbox was full of press requests from all over the world.

BH So it just exploded from there?

JH Exactly. On Monday morning we had a call from a very well-known model in New York, who said, 'Send me two pairs.' I said it was just a rendering – albeit we had the leather, we had the stitching in that model and it looked almost real. She said, 'Send me two pairs.' I realised at that point we had to make this a reality, so we got some carbon fibre and some resin and started to make our own versions.

Then we got a call from a stylist at Ann-Sofie Back, a well-known Swedish designer, to come and do her collection for London Fashion Week. And we thought, 'This is going to be real.' We really focused on making this work. At the same time we were approached by a potential future joint-venture partner, a very large shoe manufacturer that does some extremely well-known brands. They offered to invest in us to get the shoe to market. The challenge for me was to get the shoes walkable and to get the shoes to London Fashion Week and prove there was actually a demand for them.

We made ten pairs. They hadn't been walked in until they went out on the catwalk. I was nearly sick because of the pressure

'They hadn't been walked in until they went out on the catwalk, but no one fell over, and the reaction was fantastic'

that all these girls were going to walk out in these shoes that had never been tested because they had come straight from a 3D printer, then been sprayed, then been resin cast-moulded up in Cambridge. They went out, they came back in, no one fell over, no one broke a leg. It was brilliant and the reaction was fantastic and they went off to be photographed for Vogue and Elle.

At the same time, Forbes magazine ran a big article on our story. It was a feature that started with a shoe by Alexander McQueen and it talked about some Zaha Hadid work and some Sergio Rossi work and then there was a four- or five-page spread on our shoe and the link between architecture and what we're doing. It was a bit of a departure from architecture, but if you look at the shoe, it was designed, in many ways, how I would design a bridge. It's a bridge for the foot, and the foot is an integral part of the structure of that shoe.

BH How did you get the shoe made on a larger scale?

JH After Fashion Week, it was like doing an episode of Dragon's Den. My investor is a proper shoe guy and the scale of his operation is phenomenal and I'm so pleased that we found this person to work with. We've now got the full supply chain, so we have distribution set up in America, based in New York, and in Europe, based in London, and also we have an Asian distribution network.

We officially launched the product in New York in August of this year. That was the first time the shoe was taken to the market as a viable product. We came back to London and did the Pure show, then went from there to Las Vegas and Footwear News had us as one of the highlights of the show. We came back and did London Fashion Week and next week we're off to Milan for three days for a show there.

The take-up on the orders we've got is brilliant. We are so pleased with something that started as a question, an idea, an initial thought about what might happen, just because I didn't stop – I just tried it. This has also shown me how big the world is outside architecture, when you realise what one image on one website can do.

Neville Brody
'London was this thriving, humming, inspiring, exciting place to be, where anything was possible'

In this interview, filmed as part of the Design Museum's Super Contemporary exhibition, the influential graphic designer talked about the impact London's punk movement had on his work.

Marcus Fairs You have a strong connection with London. What is your relationship with the city?

Neville Brody London has always been the place that I've come back to. It's always been my base, even though in the past 20 years less than five percent of our billing and clients have been London-based. But it's always attracted creative people. And everyone passes through even though they aren't actually based here.

I went to school in north London. Then I went to the Hornsey College of Art in Crouch End, which was the birthplace of the student uprising, in 1968, and it still had that political undercurrent when I studied there, back in 1975. I then went on to the London College of Printing, as it was called. That was located in Elephant & Castle, which was probably the worst place to study. The London College of Printing was, at that time, 80 percent local printers' apprentices, with The Sun newspaper in their back pocket, practising that famous phrase, 'You can't do that, mate.'

I was there for three years doing a graphic design course. I went there to learn the basics and to understand exactly how typography is supposed to work, in terms of the rules. It happened at the same time as punk, which was probably the most influential thing to happen to me in London. The punk explosion pushed all of that out the window.

In my third year of college I moved into a squat in Covent Garden, on the corner of James Street and Long Acre. This was before the market was open. I remember there were just two or three interesting stores in Covent Garden. There was PS, Practical Styling. I think Paul Smith had just about started his first store in Floral Street. There was the Vortex club, which was on Neal Street, then the 100 Club, which was just up the road on Oxford Street.

It was a huge squat. There were maybe 150 people living there, and the whole of my first year of college was spent there. I had the whole floor across two houses, above what is now an Abbey National bank, I think. It was amazing. It was the most enthralling experience. You're right in the centre of this collapsing, decaying

Name
Neville Brody
Occupation
Graphic designer
Company
Research Studios
Location
Design Museum, London
Date
June 2009

space, post what London used to be and just prior to its rebuild as this shopping-mall experience.

The next influential place for me was Rocking Russian, which was an agency started by Alex McDowell, who's since become the key art director in Hollywood – he did Minority Report, Watchmen and he built the terminal for the Tom Hanks movie The Terminal. He does all the art direction for Spielberg's movies and Tim Burton's movies. A great old friend. He set up a studio with money from Rich Kids[1], started by Glen Matlock, who was ex-Sex Pistols. So people like Malcolm McLaren were around. Vivienne Westwood was at a certain connection distance. Alex made all the main T-shirts for the punk period, like Destroy and Fuck Art, Let's Dance, and this was all out of the same premises.

Above
The cover for 23 Skidoo's 1982 album Seven Songs, by Neville Brody

Neville Brody

1 Rich Kids was a New Wave band founded in London in 1977

2 The Face was a seminal monthly music, fashion and culture magazine, which Brody art directed from 1981 to 1986. It closed in 2004

3 Publishing company EMAP launched fortnightly pop magazine Smash Hits in 1978. It closed in 2006

It's important here to mention that the music scene in London was so vital. There were independent concerts, there was a thriving independent record label scene. And if it wasn't for that, people like myself and other graphic designers such as Vaughan Oliver and Peter Saville out of Manchester and Malcolm Garrett, we would not have survived. There would have been no support system whatsoever. This was allowing us to make a living – albeit a minimal living – but to be able to make a living pursuing ideas, explorations and having them published and put out into a public space. That was absolutely vital. London was this thriving, humming, inspiring, exciting place to be at that time, where anything was possible.

And then, out of that space, grew The Face magazine[2]. Nick Logan, who started it, had been doing Smash Hits[3] at Emap – Emap's offices were in central London, near Carnaby Street. Nick Logan had offered The Face magazine to them and they turned

'Thatcher was trying to shift culture from a thinking space to a shopping space and suppress any kind of rebellious opposition. Punk came out of that oppressive space'

it down. Nick Logan's first office was in this damp basement on Broadwick Street and I visited him there. He'd come out of a different route in London. He'd come out of the Tottenham mods. He was very much a part of the mod scene, about flashy dress, the sharpest person on the block.

This mod scene and this punk scene clashed head on and formed The Face and eventually came out as this New Romantics thing, in which I was not interested. That was a completely separate thing. I was much more interested in the industrial music scene at the time: bands like Cabaret Voltaire, down from Sheffield, and Throbbing Gristle and 23 Skidoo. I started working with 23 Skidoo because the singer was living under me in the squat in Covent Garden. So that's how I got into all that work.

London has a particular set of politics and cultural influences that has been absolutely instrumental in developing the work that

I do. There are a number of sources and ingredients for that. One is: there is such a high level of conservatism in London. When I was leaving college, Thatcher and the right wing government were pretty much running culture and trying to shift culture from a thinking space to a shopping space, and trying to suppress any kind of rebellious opposition. Punk came out of that oppressive, repressive space. It was an expression of independent individuality, it was a cry against this bland culture.

Twenty-five years later, I see we've returned to that same kind of space. And I think it's going to develop into an active, dangerous, cultural place again. So London's political and cultural space has been an absolutely vital source of thought and impetus for my work.

David Adjaye

'You can create extraordinary architectural moments across Africa with the right political environment'

London-based architect David Adjaye spent 11 years documenting every country in Africa, then collated his findings in the book Adjaye Africa Architecture. He talked to us about the project as well as future opportunities for architects working in Africa.

Name
David Adjaye
Occupation
Architect
Company
Adjaye
Associates
Location
Design Indaba,
Cape Town
Date
March 2013

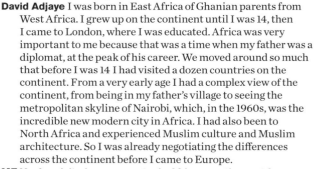

Marcus Fairs What is your relationship with Africa?

David Adjaye I was born in East Africa of Ghanian parents from West Africa. I grew up on the continent until I was 14, then I came to London, where I was educated. Africa was very important to me because that was a time when my father was a diplomat, at the peak of his career. We moved around so much that before I was 14 I had visited a dozen countries on the continent. From a very early age I had a complex view of the continent, from being in my father's village to seeing the metropolitan skyline of Nairobi, which, in the 1960s, was the incredible new modern city in Africa. I had also been to North Africa and experienced Muslim culture and Muslim architecture. So I was already negotiating the differences across the continent before I came to Europe.

MF You've visited every country in Africa over the past few years. What drew you back?

DA After graduation I realised that I wanted to revisit the continent of Africa – not through the lens of my parents, or through any kind of formal experience like tourism – but I wanted to claim it for my own, as a set of experiences that were about my negotiation of people. So I spent 11 years, from 1999 to 2010, visiting every single African country and documenting every capital to understand the nature of cities in Africa, to understand their past and their present, their history and their geography. After I did that, I realised how profoundly the geography and the history had created the contemporary condition, which is the Africa we know now. There are very extreme climates with extraordinary histories, which have created these incredible contemporary conditions. That is the lens through which you have to understand the continent. It's very difficult to understand Africa if you don't take this on board.

MF So you're talking about understanding Africa as a series of climatic zones, rather than countries?

DA Absolutely. In doing this 11-year study, what I suddenly realised is that, because of the colonial construction and the language

construction, most Africans don't even know about their neighbours, because there might be a language barrier or a geographic barrier. What became clear to me from the political map of Africa is that we have a very difficult way of understanding the continent, and that fundamentally, the way to start looking at the continent is through geography.

I started doing a lot of research on the latest satellite and data maps and extracted a map that shows the continent now. What was clear was that unlike other continents, which have some hybrid zones, Africa has six absolutely distinct unique climates. There is no cross-pollination between them.

The savanna is where the animal kingdom is. The super-dense forest is where the river deltas are, where the farm cultures are,

Above
Adjaye Africa Architecture, published in 2011 by Thames & Hudson

49

David Adjaye where the great cultures are. Then there's the mountain highland, countries like Namibia and Ethiopia. You've got the desert, which goes from Niger to Egypt. And then you have the Maghreb, which covers the Mediterranean coast and the coastal plain, with interesting vegetation that buffers the Sahara from the forest. These are where all the civilisations of Africa have manifested themselves, and their unique identities come from this.

The artefacts of the continent reflect that geography, through the choice of the materials. There are a lot of animal crafts in the savanna lands; you see a lot of timber work in the forest lands and a lot of abstract elements in the desert lands. I think this comes from human beings responding to their extreme climates very precisely, and it has created a culture and a history that are very precise.

MF Your research has now been published as a book.

DA The book is called African Metropolitan Architecture, or Adjaye Africa Architecture. It has seven volumes divided into the different geographies, plus a book of essays. I'm really proud of this – there are ultimately 11 years of work included, the analysis of all the capital cities, the architectural highs and lows, the people's relation to their geography and their political and social histories.

MF Do you have architectural projects in Africa?

DA Yes I do. I have several projects in Africa. You know me, I'm very discreet about showing my work, but I've taken a lot of things on board. We're working in the cultural sector – culture and education are areas that, again, I am most connected to. But also we're doing commercial work here. Throughout Africa there is a great need for housing, so housing is incredibly important, and masterplanning, so we've developed those skills in the office and we have started to engage with that.

We've just opened an office in Accra, which is my ancestral home. You'll see much more masterplanning and projects emerging from the Accra office that are very different from what usually comes from Adjaye Associates. So it's very important for me that we have this office, and from there I hope to be able to work more specifically on the continent.

MF What opportunities does Africa offer architects? How is it changing?

DA Africa offers an extraordinary opportunity at the moment; an opportunity and a paradox at the same time. What you have, which has been noted by various institutes, is GDP growth on the continent anywhere from ten to 15 percent, which is extraordinary. It's greater than what China was doing. But it's trickling and it's changing the political paradigm, because as people are becoming more wealthy, they are starting to question their political structure. I think you are finding the political guards shifting now, and being shaken.

But also there's the idea of the city that's being really thought through. Africa is a continent of rapid urbanisation. We had been seeing a stagnation of people moving from the agrarian landscape to the city, simply because the poor economies meant there was no need to come to the city. Suddenly with this rapid economic development, there is this mass migration into the cities, which is really traumatic. How do we plan for the expansion of these cities, which were originally built for a limited few? Most of the cities were built as small, elite centres. How do they grow while taking

'There is this mass migration into the cities, which is really traumatic'

on board the issues of their colonial past? How do they take on modern planning in light of their heritage and history? These, I think, are cosmopolitan paradoxes that the wider world is facing on a different scale. And they present fantastic opportunities. With the right political agency and the right construction environment, you can create extraordinary moments in architecture. And that, for me, is very exciting.

The kind of architecture I'm interested in seeks to make sense of environments that may seem chaotic, or programmes and ideas that seem not to have any architectural relevance but actually do. And when they are birthed, they have a profound effect on how we think and see ourselves in the world. Architecture can do that, and I'm very moved by that.

Piet Hein Eek

'In each product I try to show that materials are worth a fortune – and we're throwing them away'

The Dutch designer showed us around his studio complex in Eindhoven and talked about his thriving business turning everyday waste into covetable furniture.

Marcus Fairs You're a designer, but you also manufacture your own products here at your studio.

Piet Hein Eek I do everything – designing, making, manufacturing, distribution – everything, and as much as possible. I don't like doing one thing. It reflects very much the way I look at the task of the designer: being a generalist. If you ever have an idea and you want to realise it, you have to think about all the aspects of the idea until it reaches the consumer. If you have to think about it all, it's nice to have it in your own hands. So that's why we created the situation here where we are in control of almost every aspect of our ideas.

MF Your studio is huge.

PHE I use the word 'control' but I don't believe in controlling everything. It's more like creating an environment. If you want to do well, you've got to create an environment where you feel well. In our culture, we have much more the idea that you have a goal. There are always goals. My goal was to create this environment in order to be happy. I thought, 'If I feel good, I will function well. And if I function well, the chances of success are greater.' Then it got out of hand and got quite big.

MF What else do you do here at your studio, besides designing and making products?

PHE This is the home of our business, where we not only design but we distribute, we produce, we have storage, we have a restaurant, a gallery, we rent studios, we have an events space, a showroom and a shop. It wasn't meant to be this big. This was the only place where we could have the workshop at the heart of the organisation, which was important for us. So if a client walks in, it's possible to stand in the showroom between our products and see immediately how the products are made on the workshop floor. We had some additional square metres, so everything we wanted to do a little bit, we started doing in a really big way. The lunchroom became a restaurant. The collaboration with young designers became studios we are renting. The art above the sofa became a gallery and the little things collecting around the counter became a shop. Everything we thought was important to create our own world became very large.

Name
Piet Hein Eek
Occupation
Industrial
designer
Location
His studio,
Eindhoven
Date
October 2013

MF What was the original purpose of these buildings, before you took them over?

PHE One of the major themes in Eindhoven is Philips, the consumer electronics brand. Philips was almost the founder of Eindhoven, so the community became a city when Philips grew. Philips was all over the city in terms of buildings but also in terms of politics. When production was outsourced to countries with low-cost labour and optimised by machines and computers, Philips decreased production here. Then it left Eindhoven. It abandoned a lot of space, literally, and a lot of space, mentally, because all of a sudden the company that once had told the municipal government what to do left it to find its own way.

They also left a lot of suppliers, a lot of engineers, a lot of technicians, a lot of extremely high-end machinery, builders, everything. They left, but they created the perfect world for new initiatives. I often call Eindhoven the creative Silicon Valley of the world because it offers all the things you need as a designer. If you design, you need someone to make your design, you need the machinery, you need the technology – all those aspects were available because Philips left and the people didn't have any more work. They were also very keen on developing new ideas and new fields. The Design Academy, which was also founded by Philips, brought a lot of creative people to Eindhoven. So Philips had a very important role by leaving. That event introduced a whole new era for Eindhoven.

MF How did you find your way into design in the early days?

PHE Like I said, making something has always been the major theme. So in this little book about chairs[1], it starts with the chair I made when I was 13, with glue and rope and a little surgeon's knife. I made it with the materials I had available at that moment. That always has been the way I worked. What's available is what I work with. I'm not going to design with a machine I don't have.

I wanted to create, and I wasn't going to be a carpenter. I was able to go to university – nobody had expected that. So then it was either I become an architect or I become a designer. In the end I became a designer, but the whole theme is that I wanted to make my own stuff. When I got my degree, Eindhoven was the perfect place to produce. Only at that moment it was less obvious that it was important to realise your own designs. So I was one of the few designers who stayed in Eindhoven at that moment. These days most young designers stay here for the same reasons I stayed here 20 years ago.

MF You made a name for yourself making products from waste materials.

PHE People know me for the Scrapwood products, because when I started doing that collection, it was totally new. At a time when products were all perfect, we introduced quite a rough product.

Piet Hein Eek

We needed to make it very simple, because we produced it in Europe paying very high wages. One of the tricks to keeping it simple was to make the assembly as simple as possible, which often means you have to reveal the way it's been made. This is also a form of transparency. You can understand the product if you look at it. You'll see a bolt or a blind rivet and understand how it's been put together. So the way in which we produce and the materials we use are very important to the way the products end up looking.

It would never have succeeded if it had been slightly more expensive. I would have been unable to sell it. So in the end we had a craft-driven way of producing and distributing. We have a cupboard here called the '99.13 percent cupboard' because we aim for 100 percent material use. Even the holes to put the blind rivets into are counted as a loss. Either we make something without leftovers or we make something from the leftovers. Respect for the material, energy, technique and craft is the main issue in all my designs.

MF What other products have you developed since, and what materials do you use?

PHE We started off working with metal and wood and we have a very nice metal workshop here with all sorts of machinery. We use a lot of machines not how they are meant to be used. We put different materials in the machines because I like the materials and I like the machines and I like to have possibilities. We have ceramic products that we made ourselves in a totally ridiculous and not very efficient way. But again, if we made them in a traditional way, we wouldn't be able to compete with anyone else. We are trying to investigate totally new ways of working with ceramics. We try to develop the process instead of having our desired result as a goal.

We have a collection called Waste Waste 40 × 40. It's made from the leftovers of the leftovers. We just cut everything into 40 by 40 millimetre cubes. All of a sudden we have a size that determines the design, so the thickness of the surface is either 40 millimetres or 80 millimetres.

The thing we're working on at the moment is making stuff from garbage – rubbish from the office or the home or from travelling. On the back of the door there is a plastic bag and everything that is useless, that you normally throw away, we throw in this bag. We've made a bust out of it, a very old-fashioned application, like the Romans did. A bust is the most traditional art piece you can make, and this is to exaggerate the difference between value and garbage. Because the bust is one of the most classic themes in art. The funny thing is that you can actually see whether the piece is made of home garbage or office garbage. This is the latest step in our material fetish.

MF So this is a bust, a likeness of a human head, made out of rubbish?

PHE This is rubbish from Tenerife, so that goes under holiday rubbish. On the Tenerife beach there was a lot of plastic, and I always collect things when I'm on beaches or on holiday. The rubbish from my home has a lot of feminine things in it because I have three girls and their mother, of course. One of the girls once said, 'You can see from the rubbish that it's a women's household. It's very recognisable.'

The Tenerife beach rubbish looks very simple but it took us five times the effort to make the thing we wanted because it's like brick-laying. By piling it up, by the process, it becomes a bust. The material is very important and relevant for the shape.

Piet Hein Eek

1 The Chair, by
Piet Hein Eek,
was published
in 2012 and
features 20
years of his
chair designs

We made a huge one with tins and baskets and bins. I think it's three and a half metres high. This is a small one, but we also have busts that don't fit in this room. The way they are put together and the way they are made is very important to the way they look. In the end, it's sculpting. It's the total opposite of what we do – or maybe one step ahead.

MF How long did it take to make that?

PHE This bust took a month and a half, working every day. But we had to make it five times before we got it right. The stop-motion pictures are also beautiful because you can actually see what it takes to get the right balance in the process. It's very much learning by doing, which is also something we work on here. Though this is an extreme way of learning by doing.

MF And how much will it cost?

PHE I don't know. It's an art project and I've been working on the basic idea of it for five or six years. I made the first bust six years ago but I threw it away because I didn't like it. So if you factor in all the attempts, it would be quite expensive. But it's also meant

'Either we make something without leftovers or we make something from the leftovers'

to show the maximum difference between rubbish and value, to create the optimum, an extreme upgrade of material, which is what we do every day. In each product I try to showcase that materials are worth a fortune and we're throwing them away.

MF What's next for you? Will you keep growing until you have a bigger factory? I heard you might be thinking about making architecture.

PHE I have a lot of plans, but the main thing is that every day we're here we're happy, and every day we make a lot of stuff and get a lot of requests. I don't want to predict the future. I just like it when people come to us with strange questions that lead to new and beautiful opportunities.

In the case of making architecture, we're really fans of this building. The developer of this area thought we should take over another building nearby. Then I went to a friend of mine, who's a contractor, and we thought, 'Let's do another building.' So now we're working on three huge buildings in this area.

I always say that you have to create the circumstances where coincidence might happen. The thing we like to do is to have a nice ship with nice sails and just go out to sea. But our main focus is that we're here now.

MF You could say that your philosophy is also the spirit of the city of Eindhoven.

PHE It reflects very much also the political sense here: collaboration, creating environments, making things possible, trying new initiatives, trying to stimulate them, move them forward. That it should come out of people's own responsibility and effort is something natural here, as I've described. What we do here, we don't know what will happen, but we create the circumstances in which things might happen and that's completely different from a Western way of thinking.

We always think in goals: we want to go in here and we want to come out there, so we have to build a tunnel. We don't say, 'It should go like this, it should be planned and that will cost a lot of money.' That's not very efficient, I don't think.

Wim Crouwel
'I've always tried to be a no-nonsense designer: straightforward, readable and well-structured'

We interviewed the legendary Dutch typographer about the influences of Swiss graphic design on his career as the Design Museum launched a retrospective of his work in London.

Marcus Fairs How did you become a graphic designer?

Name
Wim Crouwel
Occupation
Graphic designer
Location
Andaz hotel,
London
Date
March 2011

Wim Crouwel I was enrolled in an art school in the north of Holland but that was a very old-fashioned school of arts and crafts and I didn't learn anything about typography or poster design – nothing. I decided to go to Amsterdam when I finished at the school.

My first little job was in an exhibition company and within a year there I learned the trade of exhibition design. While I was there I met some Swiss designers who had come to Amsterdam to take on commissions and they introduced me to the Swiss design scene of that time, in 1953 or 1954. I was highly influenced by the Swiss design scene and I tried to translate that, in my Dutch language and my Dutch way of thinking, into a specific Dutch typography.

I was lucky that the Van Abbemuseum in Eindhoven became my first large client. They gave me the freedom to do a lot of work and the director was a very good client. He only criticised me afterwards, always afterwards when the job was ready. Then he said it was a good job or a bad job. I would have loved that all my clients were that way.

When he later became the director of the Stedelijk museum in Amsterdam, I went with him and we worked for 30 years together, so he was one of my dearest clients. In 1963 we formed a design studio in Amsterdam and we were the first large design studio in the country. I stayed there until 1980 and then I left and became director of a museum in Rotterdam, which was a completely different kind of job. When I retired from that museum, I went back to designing.

MF The wallpaper and rug in this room are based on your typefaces.

WC This exhibition is very much geared to type design. I did some experimental typefaces in the 1960s and you can see some of the results here in this wallpaper, designed by Tony Brook, who also curated the exhibition. Brook reinterpreted one of my typefaces in three dimensions to give it a kind of atmosphere of space, and that turned out quite interesting. I have always done three-dimensional images in my work, especially in my graphic design, without using perspective but having an idea of space, and

Tony Brook translated that very well with a simple 'C' from my name. It's in two colours: grey and a greenish colour. The grey colour, compared with the other furniture in this room, is a perfect match.

Brook has done one of my other experimental typefaces in a carpet, here on the floor. It's a fantastic experience for me to sit with my feet on the old typefaces like I've never done before.

MF What works of yours are shown at the exhibition?

WC The exhibition was really the idea of Freda Sack from The Foundry[1], who introduced me to the staff of the Design Museum a few years ago. I had seen many exhibitions of other designers there, and when they proposed an exhibition of my work, of course I agreed. And now it's finished. I've seen it today for the

Above
Wim Crouwel with the wallpaper and carpet inspired by his typefaces

Wim Crouwel

1 The Foundry
is a typeface
library founded
in London
by David Quay
and Freda Sack

very first time. It contains almost all my work. I didn't expect that at all. I thought the show would be geared to a specific period, but they've shown almost all the work I've produced from 1952 to this day. It's amazing.

There are some chapters within it. An important chapter is about the Van Abbemuseum. In the 1960s, '70s and '80s, I did all the catalogues and posters for that museum and that's the strongest body of work in the exhibition. I'm very glad to see it work in the environment of my old work.

MF What do you consider to be your contribution to graphic design over the years?

WC You shouldn't ask me such difficult questions. I have always tried to be a designer, a no-nonsense designer – straightforward, no baroque, no fantasies, readable, with well-structured typography. That's what I've always wanted to do and I hope people remember me as a designer who was straightforward and still trying to find some tension in the work, to have work that is still recognisable.

MF What do you think are the most important objectives as a graphic designer?

WC Readability and clarity. Design shouldn't be complicated, first of all. The designer should stand between the message and the receiver. It should be neutral. It should be a good translation of

'I have always done 3D images in my work – without using perspective but having an idea of space'

the subject, so that the reader can grasp it in one eye. Not complicated: simple and straightforward work. It should also have a certain tension, be recognisable, but never stand in the way of getting out the message.

MF Of all the graphic designers you've come across in your career, who has had the greatest influence on your work?

WC My heroes were Josef Müller-Brockmann and Max Bill, both from Switzerland. They were the great masters for me – especially Müller-Brockmann. His posters were a great influence on my work and I've also gotten to know him very well. He was a very good friend. My work has even been in the latest exhibition he did in his birth town in Switzerland.

MF How do you think the digital revolution has changed graphic design and typography?

WC I was in an exhibition of print and paper in 1964 in Germany and I saw the first digital-typeface producer and the products that came out of it were horrible. They were so horrible that I thought I should design a special typeface for the digital era. That's why I designed this typeface that you see here on the carpet. It's strange. It was absolutely unreadable. But it was an experiment and I only wanted to lead the way, to say to my colleagues, 'If you think about type design, think along these lines.' It found ground in the whole direction of type design. It's very nice how they made a carpet out of it.

Craig Robins
'The one thing you can't do is replace something truly historical'

Property developer Craig Robins has helped transform Miami from a sleazy resort into a major cultural centre. He told us about his role in the regeneration of the city's Art Deco district and, more recently, the Design District.

Ben Hobson You were born here in Miami. Tell me about your relationship with the city.

Craig Robins I was born in Miami Beach and I've always lived in Miami. I went away to school, of course – spent some time at the University of Michigan and the University of Barcelona – then I came home after college and went to law school. When I was in law school, I started acquiring properties on South Beach.

BH Why did you start investing in South Beach property?

CR Initially I wanted to have a studio space so I could invite artists to paint or make art in Miami. I knew South Beach was a rundown place where perhaps I could find an inexpensive studio. I met this incredible guy named Tony Goldman[1], who became an important mentor. He had the perfect studio but told me if I wanted it, I had to buy a 50 percent interest in some buildings he owned, including the one with the studio, which I did. I began renovating one of the buildings to create storage spaces in order to afford the studio. I didn't really know anything. One of the great things about having Tony as a partner was that he gave me the freedom to do a lot of it myself but also provided guidance.

BH How did that then develop?

CR The first exciting thing was that I convinced Keith Haring[2] to open a variation of his New York store, Pop Shop, in South Beach. That was really a wonderful moment. I remember Keith at the door and he was customising things for people and there was a line down the block. There was really nothing else in South Beach at that time, so it was a great way to start. The store did really well.

BH What was South Beach like in those days? How has it changed?

CR I remember in 1982 I was in college in Barcelona and I would tell people I was from Miami and they would immediately say, 'Julio Iglesias!' Then I came home and a few years later I went back and I'd tell people I'm from Miami and they would say, 'Miami Vice!' That was their image of Miami. A few years later when I was working in South Beach and I'd tell people I was from Miami, they would think of an Art Deco building. That was an important renaissance in Miami. We had the world's largest collection of Art Deco and Mediterranean Revival structures in the same place.

But it was very rundown. It had become a retirement village for an ageing population that was dying off. There were also areas

Name
Craig Robins
Occupation
Property developer
Company
Dacra
Location
His office, Miami
Date
December 2013

that had become difficult slums. There was a crack epidemic in the US, all of which contributed to the neighbourhood spiralling downward. There were a lot of people who thought the buildings should be torn down. There was a group of us who not only thought they should be preserved but that they could become this incredible legacy that Miami could offer to the world.

So that became my career: trying to figure out how to adapt these great historical structures and put businesses that function in a contemporary way in them. It was a great time. I learned the value of design and style and doing things in a special way, because even though people didn't see it at the time, it was the unique thing Miami had. Anyone can build new buildings and if it's good architecture, that's a good thing. But the one thing you can't do is replace something truly historical. We had that going for us.

BH Was this an unusual approach to development at the time?

CR It was a big contrast to how things were done in the States. South Beach is much more European. The structures are smaller. The neighbourhood is pedestrian-friendly, which in Miami is almost nonexistent. One of the things that was really nice was working with another visionary, Chris Blackwell[3]. Chris had sold Island Records and wanted to start in hotels. He and I did a lot of investing in South Beach, opened a bunch of hotels. From Chris I learned to produce creativity because he approached real estate like a guy who made records with artists and ended up with a great creative product. That's still true for me today.

BH Which hotels did you work on together?

CR The first hotel that Chris and I did together, which is sadly not anything like it was, is the Marlin. It's a beautiful, historical structure. At the time I was living in this other magnificent building adjacent to it called the Webster.

Some of the other properties that were especially prominent were the Victor and the Tides hotels, the Cavalier, the Cardozo, the Carlyle... Some of them we developed or collaborated on with others or sold to interesting people. Gloria and Emilio Estefan bought the Cardozo from us early on and did a beautiful job with it.

Part of what we realised was that it was better for somebody else to own a property, to make their own expression, so the neighbourhood had this competitive, collaborative spirit, where everybody was expressing themselves in their own way – the opposite of what Disney World does, which is also an effective business model but its idea is to give you a fantasy with something that's fake and our business model is to do something that's real.

BH How did these hotels help transform South Beach into the hip destination it is today?

CR When I look back at South Beach, there were obviously hotels but there was no one to stay in them. There was a beautiful beach. Locals would go to the beach but people weren't flying to Miami to go to the beach. By redoing the Art Deco buildings, a lot of media came to do fashion shoots, bringing in the beautiful people, creating an industry in the neighbourhood. That began to attract more people and more life, the idea of restaurants and nightclubs. Hotels became more in demand and the need for office space for music and film things happening in South Beach increased.

These synergies came together and began to really churn in a way that was unexpected and, to some degree, uncalculated, because it was something new, a completely different approach to anchoring a neighbourhood. It wasn't like getting Marriott to build some boring hotel. It was a special place. Everything that was done in South Beach was all handmade, in a sense. They were all boutique hotels. There were no chains for years, which I think made it really cool.

BH So Miami overcame the seedy reputation and now it is emerging as a serious cultural centre. How did that happen?

CR Miami with South Beach had become known as 'fun in the sun.' The transformation from a hedonistic place that people were flying to from around the world to a city of cultural substance really happened with Art Basel[4], not just as a commercial fair but also as a cultural happening, with parties and events, with exhibitions that weren't necessarily oriented for profit.

BH And why did Art Basel come to Miami?

CR I can't speak for Art Basel but clearly it was a brilliant decision – not just because of the obvious success, but if you think about it, Basel is such a traditionally powerful, conservative city. And when you combine the solidity and power of Basel with the sex appeal and excitement of Miami, you get this amazing result that was beyond what anyone could have imagined.

BH Did Art Basel influence your decision to launch the Design Miami fair and the Design District?

CR It led to the next, somewhat contrarian innovation – that design was as collectible as art. So we founded the Design Miami[5] collectors fair, which I continue to chair. Suddenly furniture design was being collected side by side with this great art fair. It was an enormous success. People began to realise that furniture could be collected like art, so you could do these limited-edition contemporary pieces, which offer a level of freedom and experimentation, a creative approach that's different from mass-production. The Design District[5] became the place where that vision was launched, and it became more and more recognised as a cultural destination. Restaurants began to open, there were more art experiences.

BH So tell me about the Miami Design District. What is the history of the area?

CR The Design District is located in what was originally a pineapple farm. It's hard to believe, looking at the urban sprawl now. This

guy Theodore Moore, who built the Moore furniture company, built his first furniture store in the area in the '20s. It's still an unbelievable structure, not only from the exterior but when you walk into this old furniture showroom, the proportions are just perfect. Even more perfect because Zaha Hadid – she won Design Miami's Designer of the Year in 2005 – was commissioned to do Elastika, a magnificent installation inside the space. To me it's a great example of how a brilliant architect or designer can interact with a historical structure and enhance the experience, not detract from it. Elastika does that beautifully in the Moore building.

Over the years the Design District became a centre for furniture design, but by the mid '80s, as places became more and more 'mallified' in America, the district went into disrepair.

Above
The Cardozo
Hotel in South
Beach, Miami

Craig Robins

1 Tony Goldman
(1943–2012)
was an American
developer who
helped transform
the Wynwood
and South Beach
districts of Miami

2 Keith Haring
(1958–1990) was
a New York street
artist popular
in the 1980s

3 Chris Blackwell
founded Island
Records and
owned several
hotels in Miami
and the Bahamas

4 The Art Basel
annual art
fair launched
in Miami in
December 2002

BH What did you see in the area and how did you redevelop it?

CR I felt that things were becoming so commercialised in South Beach that Miami needed a creative laboratory, an important place where interesting things could happen and where the definition of what could happen was not so rigid. So part of what we did was we brought back furniture design stores. That in itself was a great challenge. It was contrary to contemporary thought at the time.

When we started in the Design District, what I found astounding was that almost nowhere in America could you see furniture design other than in a fortress-like mall. People were

'Shopping malls had a monopoly. A lot of designers didn't want design to be on the street. We took that on'

prohibited to enter if they didn't have a licence. It was treated like a prescription drug where it would maybe hurt you to see it.

The competitive malls also had a monopoly. They had a radius clause, so retailers weren't allowed to open within 20 or 40 miles of where the mall was. A lot of the designers who got commissions from the stores in the mall didn't want design to be on the street. They didn't want the client to be able to walk in and look at things. They wanted to control the environment, and we took that on.

Our great collaborator in the neighbourhood was the furniture designer Holly Hunt, who has a beautiful showroom in the Design District and is an important person in the American design industry. She was one of our first tenants, and that began a process where now you can walk around the Design District and see a lot of great furniture design. Suddenly there was business here and everything was thriving.

But I realised that design doesn't bring in people. People might buy a sofa every ten years. It's not like fashion or restaurants. So we were doing well but we didn't have a lot of people. We thought about that and said, 'This neighbourhood should really take a longer-term approach and continue with that idea of the creative laboratory. We should invest in culture, not necessarily profit and business, to continue to build the brand.'

BH Today the Design District is as well-known for its fashion stores as it is for art and furniture design. How did that come about?

CR Furniture was very successful. Restaurants were starting to open. It was then that I realised the final ingredient that was going to really catapult this neighbourhood to another level of creative offering would be if we could bring the fashion business here.

At first I got some great brands here. Christian Louboutin opened a store and said, 'I want people to walk through an art installation into the store.' I thought he was crazy. Who would go through this space into the store to buy shoes? Well, I have to say it's one of the most successful stores per square foot in Miami.

That led to other brands. So now stores are being operated or built by Vuitton, Dior, Céline, Pucci, Hermès, Cartier... Everybody is doing global flagships that are interesting expressions. I think we have a chance to be the most interesting neighbourhood in the world, with this balance of art, design, fashion and food.

BH What's next for the Design District?

CR Fashion is a powerful industry and when you combine it with the other businesses we have, it fuels the ability to do more art and design. Artists like John Baldessari and Nate Lowman are doing buildings. We commissioned a prototype from Konstantin Grcic. We're doing buildings with architects like Aranda\Lasch, Sou Fujimoto, Keenen Riley. We're getting a lot of freedom to do things.

Businesses will be more inclined to establish themselves here. The goal is to make it a great place to shop, find furniture, eat, but most importantly to just walk around. You can come here and just enjoy yourself. A lot of elements will make this neighbourhood a pleasant experience, hopefully.

BH When will the Design District reach completion?

CR It'll happen in waves, and in part that's intentional, because we don't want it to be like a mall. We want it to have new experiences constantly. Going back to the music analogy, we want to build our fan base over time: we started off in a little bar playing songs and now we're getting to bigger venues and hopefully one day we'll be in football stadiums. That's the goal.

The first phase of the Design District is complete and there are some great shops. In November 2014 there will be 15 new buildings; the Baldessari and the Grcic installations will be inaugurated. The Fujimoto building will be complete, as will this Aranda\Lasch building that will house four brands, including Tom Ford. Some of the brands are doing their own buildings and they will also be really powerful additions to the neighbourhood.

By the end of 2015 we'll probably have finished a series of condos and a boutique hotel. There will be 16 more stores, 15 buildings, retail shops, restaurants – a continual experience. There's a reason for you to come back each year for the next three years and catalogue the art, design and fashion happening.

5 Collectible design fair Design Miami was founded in 2005 and runs anually alongside art fair Art Basel

6 Robins began acquiring properties in Miami's Design District in the late 1990s

Thomas Heatherwick
'We don't work in two dimensions. We're not flat'

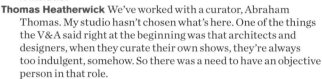

As an exhibition of his work opened in London, the British designer discussed his design for a new double-decker bus and his 'hairy' British pavilion for the 2010 Shanghai Expo.

Marcus Fairs Tell us a bit about your new exhibition. What does it include?

Thomas Heatherwick We've worked with a curator, Abraham Thomas. My studio hasn't chosen what's here. One of the things the V&A said right at the beginning was that architects and designers, when they curate their own shows, they're always too indulgent, somehow. So there was a need to have an objective person in that role.

Name
Thomas
Heatherwick
Occupation
Designer
Location
V&A Museum,
London
Date
May 2012

We've never had a show of our work. The studio has been going for 18 years. We've got a space we call an archive, but when Abraham put all the objects he wanted on the table, we were looking at it and it felt like junk. 'Are you serious? Is that going to be in the Victoria and Albert Museum?' But it's amazing what a display case can do to something. It's got this mix of being a lot about the process, so there are things I did when I was at the Royal College of Art for my graduation. There are three times as many objects here than they've ever had in this gallery, so it's all crammed in. I think the curator became interested in the workshop side of things – not just the shiny outcomes, but how we got there.

MF You've designed the cauldron that will hold the flame at the London 2012 Olympics, but it's not in the exhibition.

TH It's the most top-secret thing we've ever worked on.

MF So what can you tell us about that right now?

TH Obviously I can't tell you anything about that. But the thing is, it's not just a thing: it's a moment. It's the most public moment you can possibly do. Danny Boyle[1] is a 'moment' designer. It's been interesting trying to think of that dimension in our collaboration with him. And London's Games, after the phenomenal thing that was Beijing, what does London have? Ideas. The British government has said yes to an idea we think is quite exciting.

MF And that will be revealed on...?

TH It will be wheeled in here on 27 July, which is the night of the opening ceremony.

MF How do you approach projects? Is there a unifying thread to the objects and the projects in this room?

TH Ever since I was little, I've been interested in ideas, so I hope that's what links together this collection of projects. I've never seen these as different disciplines. I see this collection as one discipline that is designing in three dimensions. In general, we don't work in two dimensions. We're not flat.

The interest is in the world that surrounds us and why things exist – like getting a chance to work on, say, the new London bus. Everyone's become very obsessed with buildings, the power of one or two special buildings in a city. And yet if you come to London, the quantity of elevation of an art gallery or a library can't compare to the quantity of elevation of a double-decker bus. Buses are a main part of the architectural experience in London. The particularity and expression of the values of cities don't just have to manifest in the art galleries. They manifest in the infrastructure. And in fact I believe it's more interesting to focus on improving infrastructure.

MF Part of one of the new double-decker buses you've designed is here in the exhibition.

TH The last time a design team was allowed to work on London's buses was 50 years ago. London's famous for its red buses and yet, in my opinion, the experience has been degraded as different health and safety laws and regulations have come in. The only requirements London's transport authority has had for so long have been: double decker, make it red. Other than that, different operators, because they're not owned by London's transport authority, have been able to say: all the fabric is purple with yellow spots. Okay, you want a chiller? Just put that big lump of chiller above the stairs, blocking everyone's view with a mysterious lump. Our job is to bring together all those European directives and best-practice issues and make it not feel that it's a collection of compromises.

The key aspects of the brief were to make a bus that uses 40 percent less energy than the diesel buses you see and also to improve the reliability. That romantic notion of a bus that people love and think of in London has one door, and that means you're waiting for all the passengers to unload before the passengers waiting at the stop can load up. If there are a lot of people, that can take a long time. That means the timetable will be very unreliable. So having three doors and two staircases means you can load and unload much faster, and it means the bus is more likely to meet its schedule.

Also, the bus that people are romantic about when they think about London, you can't get a wheelchair on it, or the modern baby buggies. There are different needs now, 50 years later, and we're trying to manifest them in a bus.

The back of the bus is like the end of a loaf of bread. The reason for rounding it was to try and reduce the perceived brickiness. The effect is reminiscent of the original London Routemasters. The bus itself is three metres longer than the old Routemaster. It's huge.

**Thomas
Heatherwick**

The intention wasn't to remake something from the past; we've not tried to reinvent ideas that don't need reinventing. One of the most basic examples of that was the bus seat. At the moment, you get into a bus and your eye is bombarded by all these plastic buckets. Each one has a handle and a crevice that a crisp packet can get caught in. We've reintroduced a bench seat that is just one element, one handrail across the back, so your eye is calm when you're in that environment.

Using darker colours on the lower part and lighter colours on top is a funny thing. We had to make the bus look good dirty because the bus is cleaned only once a day. On a slushy winter's day when 70 school kids get on, the floor is going to get slushy and sandy and the seats might have a bit of kebab or whatever on them. So we developed distortion patterns. We designed a repeat that was the size of the body and the distortion pattern is the same shape as your body, a bit like contours.

The bigger thing is that the bus has two staircases. And what the Mayor of London really wanted was an open platform. You're not a prisoner in the bus when it's three metres from your stop. You can get on and off. The meanest bit about the old staircases was going up through a solid plastic tube. It just seemed a basic thing that you could get a view of London as you circulate. So here, there's this staircase that sweeps around and the glass sweeps around the back. At the front it's the same. The daylight pulls you through.

MF One of your best-known projects is the 'hairy' UK pavilion from the Shanghai Expo 2010.

TH In Shanghai we won the competition to represent, or somehow communicate, Britain at the world's largest Expo. We had half the estimated budget of the other Western nations. There were going to be 250 pavilions there, more than you could see even if you spent four months there. But we were told, 'You've got to be in the top five.' That was in the British government's brief. That was the most useful bit of the brief. We had no context to work with because all the other pavilion designers around the world were thinking about the same thing at the same time. So we had to try and second guess what the trend might be.

We tried to focus on not being a cheesy advert for Britain: umbrellas and bowler hats, the Queen, David Beckham. I just thought, 'Well, what might have more meaning?' So we thought we'd show something that Britain has never seen either. It came back to saying one thing. And if we could just say one thing, with our little half-budget, we could really stand out.

Everyone had a site the size of a football pitch. If we'd spent our budget making a football pitch-sized building, we wouldn't have had any money left for content. So we only used a sixth of the site, and within the surrounding public space we had all the

government meeting spaces and broom cupboards and staff training rooms and toilets. By making it only a sixth of the site, you suddenly get the perception of proportion. This 'seed cathedral' was the outcome of that thinking.

The Expo was about the future of cities. And what came up in our research was that London, for its sheer size, is the greenest city in the world, with public parks, gardens, squares and the world's first botanical institution, Kew Gardens. The seed bank that Kew has set up, near Gatwick airport, is an incredible project that few people have ever seen, but some of the seeds are beautiful. We went to see the head of the seed bank and they agreed to give us a quarter of a million seeds. The whole project depended on that.

**Thomas
Heatherwick**

1 The film
director Danny
Boyle directed
the opening
ceremony for
London's 2012
Olympic Games

2 Thomas
Heatherwick:
Making was
published in
2012 by Thames
& Hudson

The space is made from 66,000 fibre-optic rods. You could say each is a vitrine or a window. Each fibre-optic rod is embedded with a sample of seeds at the tip. The building is a box punched with 66,000 holes for these fibre-optic rods and seeds and then waterproofed. The building moved in the wind and it's the only project we've done that looks more like a render than the render.

The surrounding space did a couple of jobs. People were exhausted from walking around the Expo, so it gave them the chance to sit down on a piece of landscape that wasn't just flat, that brought people together. We developed, with an artificial grass manufacturer, a micro version of the pavilion surface. It was silvery and soft and because it was soft, it absorbed sound, so there was this underlying silence. It was just like when it snows.

MF Do you think of yourself as a British designer? In your book[2] you mention your engineering heritage, from your grandfather, and your influences. Is there a notion of Britishness that you express, or is it just by chance that you're working in London?

TH As a country that was the first to industrialise, that has such a cultural accumulation, I feel like I was very lucky I was brought up in London. I haven't had to think where I should be in the world. It's had a gravitational pull and I think that it's loose and scraggy enough as a city that it makes people feel comfortable to be here – as well as having these incredible institutions like the

'The Olympic cauldron is not just a thing: it's a moment. It's the most public moment you can possibly do'

V&A. I do find it amazing that you can get on a bicycle and in 25 minutes be at the front door of some of the most talented people in the world. Those aren't necessarily people who were born in Britain but people who have chosen to base themselves here. Designing the pavilion in Shanghai, I felt a kind of duty to represent the phenomenal people and imagination based in Britain. If the pavilion had turned into a cliché, it would really not be reflecting a true picture.

MF Can you tell us about your Christmas cards, because I think this is the thing I love the most, especially when I get one. Tell us about the dilemma of sending Christmas cards as a designer.

TH When I was little, my family made cards for one another. Nobody bought a pack from WHSmith, which already had the message

written in, where you just put 'Dear John' or 'Dear Bob'. It got
a bit out of hand and carried on into adult life. I set up the studio
18 years ago, and you need a lot of help to begin with, whether
that's people giving you advice or showing you how to do things,
or lending you things. When trying to say thank you, I didn't have
any money to give anyone the obvious thing, like a bottle of
whisky. What I did have was the ability to give an idea. I'm sure
many people would rather have had a bottle of whisky, but it felt
like the thing you could give that was more unique. So for 17
years we did our own cards. Our first-ever Christmas card is
in the V&A's collection.

MF What's that card like?

TH The card was looking at what's the least you could possibly send
someone. Well, you've got to send the stamp. So here the person's
address is written on the back of the stamp, and there's a little
greeting on there. It's trapped in a block of acrylic, a bit like ice,
but we imagined it getting pushed through the letterbox, and the
dog going to get the letters and choking on this thing.

   I got interested in the process of posting because a key part
is it's not about spending money. It was expending the effort
on something. We made friends with the big sorting office near
our studio in King's Cross, with a man who runs the special
hand-stamp centre, and each year they'd work with us to make
that card happen. So the stamp on this one is floating in the
block and even the postmark is floating. In a way it was part of
the festiveness within the studio, making the cards. Sometimes it
was as hard as designing a building. It was a very tight project
because it can't weigh a certain amount or you'll have to pay for
first-class stamps, and you'd rather pay for second-class stamps.
It was a tight little piece of product design.

Winy Maas

'We didn't come all the way from the Netherlands just to make a copy of a barn'

The Dutch architect talked to us about MVRDV's Balancing Barn, a holiday home that cantilevers dramatically over a hill in the English countryside.

Marcus Fairs The philosopher Alain de Botton was your client. How did he approach you?

Name
Winy Maas
Occupation
Architect
Company
MVRDV
Location
Balancing Barn,
Suffolk, UK
Date
November 2010

Winy Maas Actually, we were approached by Mark Robinson from Living Architecture[1] to develop one of their holiday homes in the UK. The homes are all designed by different contemporary architects, and are places where all kinds of people can go to experience contemporary architecture.

It was initiated by Alain de Botton. Alain is a successful writer, a philosopher and a documentary filmmaker. He made a documentary on architecture and everything that surrounds the experience of architecture, as well as writing The Architecture of Happiness, a well-known book about what he thinks architecture should do.

He's a very philosophical person and not only an observer but also one who wants to go one step further. And that's a very attractive client, in a way, partly because he sets a tone, architecturally and historically, and he has a frame of reference, because of his writing, of what architecture should do. That can be very intimidating. Normally architects are not so eloquent. They are more into making.

That challenge is what we took up and the building is answering that element. It also makes a story. It becomes a narrative with highlights and drama. Having phone calls and trying to explain the value of certain issues and talking for two hours on the phone – you can see that in the building in the end, because architecture should describe that.

MF What was the idea behind Balancing Barn?

WM The Balancing Barn is a building that wants to laugh at folk culture and wants to criticise the act of being on vacation. Living Architecture wants to make people experience holiday homes in different ways. They asked us, 'What can you add to that conversation?'

Alain de Botton and Mark Robinson together selected this site, which is a cliché of Suffolk, the British landscape of hedges and frogs. It's slightly hilly, with barns of slightly different natures on it. The selection of that particular site was the starting point of the operation.

The Balancing Barn is already a name that deals with that cliché, in that way, because it was kind of an intuitive reaction to the most picturesque of all the spaces Living Architecture had to offer at that moment. We were confronted with the National Trust[2] and the parks committees and the environmental committees very strongly, so when I look back at the last three years, I spent more time talking about the building than, say, constructing it. It says something about the care as well as the traditional attitude that surrounds the British landscapes we were confronted with.

I remember we worked on a concept for Stonehenge for a while, to get a commission for the visitor's centre. We were opposed because we were too strong and the idea was that we couldn't match the Stonehenge image. This is, in a way, a kind of revenge on that. The building wants to deal with that love affair but it wants to bring it one step further.

We started with no house, a house that disappears, but that became technically very confusing. Everyone wanted to simply have a barn, so we accepted a barn. You could reject such a thing as an architect, become too proud or whatever. But we said, 'No, let's take it seriously.'

Immediately, though, we said, 'We didn't come all the way from the Netherlands just to make a copy of a barn.' So it became a starting point for what you can do with that issue. We said, 'Well, you put a barn on top of the hill. It's there.' But the moment you push the barn a little bit out over the hill, or even a bit more, then the barn gets an emotional feeling, in a way. It starts to be not completely comfortable. It is comfortable initially, but then you go further in the house and you see there's no soil below.

A home should not be boring. It should distract you from city life and it should comfort you in a certain way, but that is such a cliché. So we thought this would be a good starting point. The house, in a way, becomes floating.

It has the smallest footprint, which was part of the negotiations: a small footprint so frogs can pass by. But it is also big in a way. It's still a house that grandma can go into. It has two ends. Sleeping is in the heart but the two balancing ends are the collective zones, for living or writing or reading or cooking.

We discussed what it should look like. Do we do a real copy of the barns that are around here? Barns from the nineteenth century that are made of wooden sticks with infill? They have chicken farms and barns that are basically sheds. Somewhere in

'It's like a Magritte painting. You don't know exactly what it is, so it enlarges the story'

between, this building starts to behave in negotiation with that environment. We could have copied a stone barn, but we thought, 'No. We'll plant mirrors, so when you're there, you will see that it's heavy but on the other hand, it reflects nature.' It's like a Magritte painting. You don't know exactly what it is, so it enlarges the story.

When you visit a house you see a story, you want to be its friend, you want to come into a house that has a story. When you start with no house, you have to write that story. I think that answer to our client was very eloquent. Alain de Botton has incredible thoughts about architecture, has written excellent books on it, so in that way it was intimidating, as an architect, to respond with a kind of storytelling. In the end, that's ultimately what the house is.

There was a moment in the discussion when it was too expensive. So we worked on the reduction of the size of the house, on finding a structure that would be cheaper. So now it's simply a steel truss. We started to accept the consequences, in a way. We discussed, 'Should we have the barn balance and then have a stone on the end to compensate for this, to keep it down?' But that's too obvious.

It led to an interior that's dominated by the steel structure. Then we thought, 'No, no, we also want to make a love affair with the country house. It should be domestic. So let's clad everything.' All the interior steelwork we simply clad with timber wood and plywood and suddenly you get a sculpture. And then it becomes domestic as well, because of the simple wood. You get shapes of cupboards that you can put things in. Books can be placed like this or notes can be hung up there. That combines this domestic feeling with the expression of the story in the structural components of the building.

Then we asked Jurgen Bey, a Dutch designer who is able to work with domesticity, 'Can you go further with it?' And there the story continues. He didn't make only one bed, he made different beds. So every room has a different bed. We asked him, as well, for every room to share something with the landscape, so he made paintings and pixelated them in different ways. He collected different plates and cutlery, so that if you are there, you can choose which plates you want to put out. So even when something falls, it's not a problem. You buy another set of plates and you add it to the collection. So he expanded the storytelling in the building.

MF Is there any secret to the structure? How does it stay up?

WM The structure was developed with a very good structural engineer. Basically the whole house is a hollow beam. The hollow beam can hold itself up, but not enough. It has to be pushed down to the ground before it can cantilever out. That pushing act is done by a huge block of concrete anchored to the hill that stabilises this hollow beam. The house is basically balancing on a huge panel made of concrete, which is landscaped, so you don't see it. Because we're talking about a very respectful landscape. The block keeps the house up in the end.

The house was essentially created from a 3D steel truss that looks like a bridge. We built it in steel and clad it completely in wood to make the steel invisible, so you could start to love it.

Winy Maas

1 The not-for-profit holiday home rental company Living Architecture was founded by philosopher Alain de Botton

2 The National Trust for Places of Historic Interest or Natural Beauty is a conservation organisation in the UK

MF How does the cantilevered structure affect the way people experience the building?

WM The house wants to appear modest. It wants to respect the landscape. It's simply a barn, in a way, and the barn is positioned at the end of a small avenue that was already there initially. They wanted to get rid of the trees, but we wanted to keep these apple trees and put the house at the end of that avenue.

When you approach the house, you come from the main road. You go into this alley and there you suddenly see the house. Imagine you have to drive for two and a half hours from London, you have to pass 60 roundabouts, you are getting to hate that landscape already and then you have to come into the house. You only see a small house but then, actually, you see yourself, because the mirrors reflect you. It has the classic shape of the Suffolk barn, modest but also reflective.

Because of the shiny material, the barn is dominated by the moon and even the stars. You park your car, you suddenly wonder, 'Where's the door?' Of course, there's not one door, there are actually two doors. But you go around the house to search and it looks like just a barn. You go further and it's still a barn, then further and suddenly you're in this gap and the barn seems to leave the ground, so you go back immediately, enter the house and check the interior.

Immediately you're in the kitchen. I love that in a house – that you don't go through a hallway. After the kitchen you come immediately into an intimate zone, a set of bedrooms, like a hotel, except every room is different.

Further, further, further, and then – poof – you come into the library. And then you realise that what you've seen outside is actually floating, actually happening. There are windows on the sides and on the ends to watch the landscape. You can see the night, the stars, but also the floor is made out of glass. So you look down, and what do you see? A swing, the landscape, the frogs. So the ultimate 3D experience of Suffolk can be found there. That's the secret of the house.

MF The house has a lot of windows and skylights.

WM The interior of the house is simply wood – light wood, not a dark wood. You can look at any piece of this simple wooden interior sculpture during the day. All the windows are opposite one another. They are like beams of light that bring you from one step to the other. When you are in the beam of light, you can look out at the two sides of the landscape, so the house becomes like an X-ray, almost. On both ends of the house there are two big windows and two doors.

During the day, that's clear. But what to do with the night? Normally I hate artificial lights. So we added skylights where possible, over every bathroom, so you can lie in your bath and look

up at the rain. The same over the toilet. In the night, those are places where, when you open the door, the moonlight comes in. So skylights are not only useful during the day but during the night as well. You are in your bed, you don't want to put on the lamp and wake up your kids, but you can find the toilet anyway because it's lit by natural light.

Alexandra Daisy Ginsberg
'You could build circuits out of DNA and you can programme living matter'

Designer Alexandra Daisy Ginsberg collaborates with scientists working in the field of synthetic biology. In these two interview excerpts she discusses potential future uses for this new technology and what the implications might be.

Marcus Fairs What is synthetic biology?

Alexandra Daisy Ginsberg Synthetic biology is a new approach to genetic engineering. Engineers have come into biology and said this can just be another material for making stuff. I heard about it first about five or six year ago, and as a designer I was really intrigued by how biology could be a material to make things. The idea is to make biology like computer science: you could build circuits out of DNA and you can programme living matter.

MF Are you saying we can redesign the natural world?

ADG We've been designing biology for at least 10,000 years. Everything, from crops to your pet dog, has been designed. It's been iterated and iterated by human decisions until it's become the thing we want. The idea behind synthetic biology is that we can get far more control and start moving things across living kingdoms that haven't necessarily interacted at a genetic level before. So an antifreeze gene from a fish could be put into a tomato to make it cold-resistant. That's something that genetic engineering has done, but with synthetic biology you could imagine putting pigments from different coloured vegetables into bacteria and it starts to create whole new opportunities. You could have new materials and unlimited fuel and all sorts of things that society can see as desirable.

MF What work have you been doing in this area?

ADG I've been working with synthetic biology in different ways. Back in 2009, I started working with a team of undergraduate students from the University of Cambridge who were entering this big competition called the International Genetically Engineered Machine competition, or iGEM, where thousands of students from around the world get together to design a bacteria that does something cool. We were working with students from Cambridge who were designing bacteria that produced different coloured pigments. We were also working with another designer, James King, trying to bring the way we think about design into their design process.

We imagined that by about 2039 it would become culturally acceptable to drink a yogurt-type drink, like Yakult, laced with

Name
Alexandra Daisy Ginsberg
Occupation
Designer
Location
Design Indaba,
Cape Town
and London
Date
March 2013 and
November 2013

bacteria called E. chromi that would detect diseases in your gut. If you had a disease, the bacteria would start producing a corresponding coloured pigment. The output was easy: coloured poo. That was the thing everyone has taken from this project as a new kind of interface for biological computing.

MF Didn't you present a suitcase full of coloured poo at the iGEM conference?

ADG We wanted to challenge the scientists and the engineers who invented the technology with what we thought would be an interesting aesthetic response. They're representing it as cogs and machine parts. But this is biology and we shouldn't be coy about talking about what's unique about this technology. Because if this isn't what we want from a technological innovation, then what do we want from it?

The Scatalog, which is what we called this suitcase, is quite simple. We imagine the bacteria would be in a yogurt drink, you would buy it in the supermarket, you would drink it and what's in the suitcase is a mock-up of what your poo might look like.

We next caught up with Ginsberg in November 2013 in London, where she told us about another synthetic biology project she'd just completed.

Marcus Fairs Tell us about your new project.

Alexandra Daisy Ginsberg This project is called the Sixth Extinction. It was commissioned for Grow Your Own: Life After Nature, an exhibition about synthetic biology at the Science Gallery in Dublin. We're investigating the relationship between biodiversity, conservation and synthetic biology. Some conservationists argue that at the moment we are undergoing the sixth extinction period. So the dinosaurs dying out was one of the extinction periods, and number six is being caused by humans: the death of creatures and biodiversity.

I went to a conference at the beginning of this year called the Future of Nature, where the conservation community came to the synthetic biology community and said, 'We need to talk. Can we actually design organisms that could help biodiversity?' I was really interested in how this could be a design brief in itself – in making this relationship clearer.

In this future scenario I'm looking at how we could do 'rewilding' using synthetic biology. The idea is that we could preserve or maintain a state of nature using synthetic organisms that are designed to save other species. There are four different species that would potentially be designed by scientists and patented by corporations, maybe as part of biodiversity offsetting, so the companies that are damaging environments somewhere else are releasing these things to preserve nature.

Alexandra Daisy
Ginsberg

ADG These [pointing at an image of a slug] are bioremediating slugs that reduce acidity levels in the soil to make it more hospitable. Soils get really acidic due to pollution, but the trails of these slugs are very alkali-heavy and neutralise the soil.

These puffball-type mushrooms are actually membrane pumps that would suddenly erupt on a tree that has been infected with the pathogen that causes sudden oak death. They're very carefully designed pumps that inject serum into the tree.

These little creatures, like porcupines or hedgehogs, are mobile seed-dispersers. Their rubbery spines help catch seeds in their fur and disperse them around. In the distance you see that some of the leaves are yellowish: that's a film-like infection on the trees that's trapping glutens.

The idea is to ask whether we could design organisms like we design products in order to save nature. In the exhibition, all the organisms are described with patent application descriptions,

'We could preserve nature using synthetic organisms that are designed to save other species'

so it's very instrumentalised. We don't talk about these as living things; they're really machines. They're opening up that whole space that hasn't really been explored, about what it might be like to preserve while inventing.

MF In this scenario, how do these creatures come into being?

ADG They've been invented in a laboratory: designed, tested and released. I've designed them to work in closed ecological ecosystems. Under the patent applications you see that each one has a kill switch, so it can only copy itself a number of times before it dies.

MF So they can't take over?

ADG No. The idea is that we would have this perfect synthetic nature existing, one to save the other. Whether that's actually possible is up for debate.

MF How plausible is this?

ADG A scientist I showed this to said it's already happening – not at the organism level but with bacteria being released into nature to preserve it. She said I was too close to reality. I'm not proposing this as the future, but as a vehicle to highlight these questions. Now the idea is to take it back to scientists and start the conversation.

MF This scenario is about the natural world, but what about the human world? Could we conceivably invent creatures that look after us?

ADG There is research already going on into bacteria that can store data like hard drives. It's never going to compete with a silicon computer but it can go into a completely different space, like our bodies. The therapeutics of the future would be mini biological hard drives that can actually count how many times your cells divide, to work out if you have cancer.

We already eat so much that is genetically modified that we don't even know about. If you're a vegetarian, you're eating GM all the time because probiotics are produced by bacteria. This is not a hidden new world. It's actually happening.

Above
A slug-like mobile bioremediating device that emits alkali to neutralise acidic soil

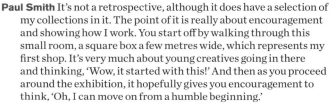

Paul Smith

'Don't look at what other people are doing. It's like buying yesterday's newspaper. It already exists'

At an exhibition of his work at London's Design Museum, the British fashion designer talked us through his career of more than 40 years.

Dan Howarth Can you tell us about the show?

Paul Smith It's not a retrospective, although it does have a selection of my collections in it. The point of it is really about encouragement and showing how I work. You start off by walking through this small room, a square box a few metres wide, which represents my first shop. It's very much about young creatives going in there and thinking, 'Wow, it started with this!' And then as you proceed around the exhibition, it hopefully gives you encouragement to think, 'Oh, I can move on from a humble beginning.'

Name
Paul Smith
Occupation
Fashion designer
Location
Design Museum,
London
Date
November 2013

Then you come to a room that is a little bit of my very crowded office in Covent Garden, and that's very much about showing that you can find inspiration from anything. It could be from things that are small and big, or rough or smooth. Then you go into this area called Inside Paul's Head. It's nicknamed the Paracetamol Room because by the time you come out, you need a paracetamol. It's full of video screens. It's quite clever how it's been done: it might show a flower and then the flower abstracts and suddenly the flower becomes a handbag or a purse. Again, it's to say: look and see and try to get inspiration from anything around you.

The next room is a bedroom, which we've hand-painted and made out of wood. It's actually based on a bedroom I stayed in in 1976 in Paris, where I showed my first tiny collection. I think it was six shirts, two pieces of knitwear and two jackets. I put some black fabric on the bed, laid out the things and then it suddenly became a showroom. I sent out some invitation cards to various people I had met over the years and nobody came. Monday, Tuesday, Wednesday, nobody came. Then on Thursday, when I was leaving, one person came at four o'clock, so I was in business. I had suddenly started. That is very much about encouragement and the fact that when you're starting out, you could have a great show at college and maybe you're taken up by a big company, or you could possibly start by yourself, but you've got to be very patient and aware. You've got to earn some money by doing some mundane jobs and have the purity of your dream.

The following room is fabulous for visitors because it's a reproduction of part of the studio, so it's full of drawings and paintings and yarn and ideas about where a collection can come from. It's divided into three parts. One is the design area, where we design the shape of the clothes. The next is the area where we choose colour. For instance, there's a beautiful book from 1904 with a print of a flower and it shows how that print develops into a fabric for a dress. So it's saying: use your eyes. Don't just look at what other people are doing or magazines or shops, because it's like buying yesterday's newspaper. It already exists. Try and be yourself, try and stimulate your brain by looking and seeing.

The next part of that room is about print. I've got lots of lovely vintage books. I scanned a rose from one of the books, sliced it up with a scalpel, scanned it again and then that became a print for a dress and for shirts for women.

If you turn around in that room, you'll see the area that is all to do with graphic design: promotional advertising, lookbooks and packaging done by famous photographers and graphic designers like David Bailey, Mario Testino, Julian Broad and many more. There's one section about my photographs because I've been taking photographs since I was 11. My dad was an amateur photographer and the camera he bought me when I was 11 is on the wall. I shoot all our advertising and promotional material now and I work for lots of magazines as a photographer as well.

Carrying on, you go to the area called 'collaborations'. There are designs for bicycles, Leica cameras, Evian water bottles, Burton snowboards, Pinarello bikes, the famous MINI I did. It's a fabulous area, really exciting, and seeing them all together is sort of, 'Oh, wow, we've done quite a lot over the years.'

Turning right, you'll see a wall covered in 70,000 buttons. It took so long to do! And there are photographs of a small sample of the many shops I have around the world, which is really all about individualism. It's my passion to make sure all the shops are different. None of them are repeated.

You turn right again and you see a long white corridor. That is where there's an example of the clothes, from the earliest ones right up to the present day. They're grouped not chronologically but by colour, inspired by colour, inspired by travel, inspired by Britishness and print.

The final room we've done with Sony's new 4K high-definition TVs and it's incredible – you almost feel like you could put your hand in the screen. It's a day in the life of a fashion show. It's my last show for men, with a commentary. You walk out of there and the central corridor is full of some of the artworks I've got in the basement of my office in Covent Garden. You'll see photographs by famous people, drawings by six year olds, masses of things. You could spend five hours in this room. You leave and on the wall it says, 'Every day is a new beginning,' and the whole idea is that you come, you get inspired and then you go out there and the next day starts the rest of your life.

Name
Arik Levy
Occupation
Industrial
designer
Location
Design Miami,
Miami
Date
December 2008

Arik Levy
'When I meet a new client, I have to feel like I'm water. I have to take the shape of the place'

As part of a series of live interviews at Design Miami, the Israeli designer showed us a slideshow of inspiring imagery and discussed his versatile approach to design over the years.

Marcus Fairs How did you become a designer?

Arik Levy I moved from Israel in 1988 to Switzerland, where I completed my studies. Then I moved to Paris for two years, 17 years ago, so things were not really in control in a way. Maybe that's the beauty of everyday experience. For me, design is a non-controlled matter. I don't think you become a designer. I did not become one. I just woke up and got lost and it's part of what I do.

MF What are you most proud of having achieved in your career?

AL After many years of hard work, I've got my own office. I don't pay rent. I think the biggest achievement I've had so far is that the office belongs to me and I take three and a half months' vacation a year, every year, for 15 years. I think that's really important.

MF Dezeen recently wrote about your Transition line of sportswear, which was a departure for you. Tell us about that.

AL It's made with one of the most amazing fashion manufacturers of high-end sportswear in Korea: Kolon. They called me a couple of years ago, selected me from an amount of people and said, 'We want you to design a brand.' And I said, 'You understand you're taking a risk because it's not my business.' I don't know how to make a pattern and I had to learn a lot. They said, 'We know and we would like to take that risk.' It was the most amazing experience I've had in the past few years. The moment when it really happened, we presented our concepts, designed the brand, the collection, the future language and the way it's going to be.

We had a meeting with 12 people in the room. Everybody speaks Korean, one translator. Nobody knows what's going on. The manufacturing department says something to someone, who says it to the guy next to me, who says, 'Not possible.' And I say, 'Why?' And he says, 'Not possible.' I asked everybody to leave the room except the head of development and manufacturing, and we are two hours in the room, not speaking the same language, just drawing and showing. Two hours later everybody came back and the translator said, 'Possible.' This was how it was born, and it was ongoing. We just started the Spring/Summer 2009 line.

MF Let's look at the first of your slides, which is a movie.

AL Sparkler is one of the films I made. It's very beautiful and it's very important to me and I think it's an important thing for everyday

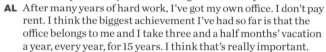

life. The 'sparkler' is a social code. When you have the sparkler
in your hand, you are happy. Everybody smiles. Nobody cries. It's
great and kids enjoy the sparkler until the end. They don't plan,
as we do. When it gets to the middle we know it's going to end. We
decide to prepare ourselves mentally. But the kids will see the end
and go, 'Ha ha, another one!'

But in fact every micro-explosion is pyrotechnics. That's the
reason why it's hot. We say the sparkler is a cold fire but it isn't.
So we start to get joys out of explosions. It's about perpetuation,
it's about hope. Every time we light another sparkler we're happy
again. I think the profession I practice is about that, too. I'm
constantly looking for midwives to give birth to a new one, to hope
that this baby is going to grow and become a product, to hope that
the manufacturer will ask for another baby, for insemination to
happen again. It's a very important thing.

MF Does the place you come from have any relevance in what you
do? Or do you see yourself as more of a universal person?

AL I think the cultural identity of each one of us is an influence for us
and it's part of our DNA. Israel is a country in war for many years.
It's a difficult place. It forces you to reinvent yourself every day.
You have to go beyond yourself every second, every day, every
morning. The extreme situation at present makes you do things
that you've never done before.

MF So it influences your approach to your work rather than the
actual work itself?

AL It could be that, but again it's a non-controlled thing. You have
to wake up in the morning and check whether it's raining or not.
Everything changes constantly. You have to be ready to change
course at any moment and also to create a new network of
surviving, still doing what you like doing. That's the challenge.

MF Your next slide is an image of water.

AL What is more beautiful than water? It's one element that takes the
shape of its container. When it freezes it will explode. It's hard and
soft, it's beautiful, it's threatening, it's deadly. Water is fantastic,
water is everything I love. I think it represents a lot of what I do.

MF Can you give us some examples of how water influences your
design work?

AL When I go to a first meeting, I have to feel like I am water. I have to
take the shape of the place, I have to take the shape of the motion,
the ergonomics, the feelings that come through and I have to
be able to explode, too. These metaphors are following me and the
people in my studio when we work. Going surfing, being before
sunrise in the water and feeling that. It's powerful.

MF I really like these tales that you tell about your work processes.
Maybe you should write a design management book.

AL That would be interesting. In the old-time business schools,
doing different things would create a crisis because you would

have to learn. They would say, 'No, concentrate. Be a car designer, be a chair designer,' and so on. In the contemporary world, in the flexible world, it's a total adventure because you import and transport from the different places you're working in – from contemporary dance to theatre to consumer electronics. And we take consumer electronics and put them in art and put art in fashion, and so on.

MF You work in contemporary dance, but do you dance?

AL Very badly, though I'm quite flexible. I worked since 1986 in contemporary dance, doing stage design and lighting, working all around the world. I think it's the most wonderful of the performing

'Israel is a difficult place. It forces you to reinvent yourself every day'

arts. You have the body, music, light, speech, colour. People can appear and disappear, become somebody else. It's a fantastic place, where the audience is putting itself in a hypnotic situation to see and receive.

MF You are a very versatile designer: clothing, set design, industrial design... What does design mean to you?

AL I think the word 'design' has taken a completely different curve. Twenty years ago you had to say you were an industrial designer. It would be understood. Radios and consumer electronics. Today you say industrial design and you're asked, 'So what do you do?' I think it's very wild and very brave, it's great. I think the platform around us is a result of huge efforts in pedagogy, in schooling, training and moving in the world from modular to flexible.

MF Let's move on and look at your next image.

AL That's a blur, representing fear, insecurity, love. Love has many different parameters. One of them is fear. This image is part of the photography work I do. It says you're not sure if there's an earthquake, or you didn't put on your glasses, or you're tired. It's a language. Since I can't write, I speak in this way.

MF Your final image?

AL This is a bench, a beautiful bench that I want to cast in bronze. If anyone wants to offer me the money for that? A sponsor? No? It's a typical construction bench that you can find on every construction site in Israel. I haven't seen it in any other place. These benches would be the first things to come onto the site. Then the building will start. The workers are going to use this

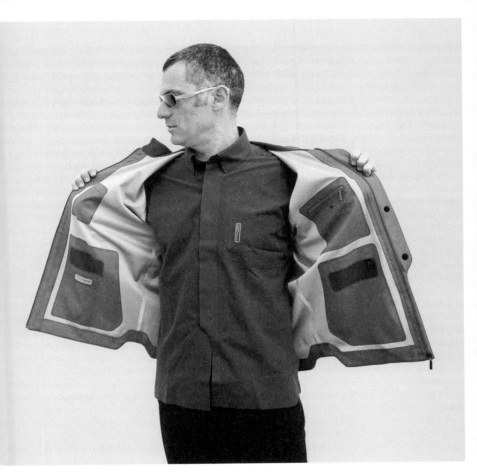

bench to have lunch and talk and work. The bench is going to live the life of the span of time it takes to build. The beauty of it is how old and how many hammer hits and the quantity of cement that's fallen on it... It's a real trace of life, the beauty of usage.

People talk about perfection. When we make a stainless-steel object, people will ask us, 'Will it scratch?' Of course it will scratch. But the beauty of a scratch is that it is a moment in life. It is a memory. You are going to remember this scratch. And everybody else will too.

Above
Arik Levy wearing a jacket from his 2007 Transition collection for Kolon Sport

Marc Newson

'My vision of the future is one of great simplicity and great elegance and, dare I say it, better taste'

The Australian designer flicked through a copy of his latest monograph with us at his London studio, touching on some of his favourite projects from the vast body of work he's produced over the years.

Marcus Fairs Why did you want to do this book?

Marc Newson It's not the first book I've done. It's probably the fourth. Some have been complex, some less complex. But I really wanted to do something incredibly comprehensive that described what I really do, how I started working, where I started and why I started, why I'm interested in techniques and materials. Why I'm interested in different industrial processes, and also describing the way I get an idea from my head into reality. It goes through several iterations and steps along the way.

MF Has the way you work changed over the years?

MN To be honest, it's changed a lot. In the early days of my career, design was kind of a hobby. Now it's very much a job, so the dynamic has changed. Rather than a leisurely process, whereby ideas would just sort of come into my head, now I really have to apply myself and attempt to solve problems in a far more proactive way.

MF What set you off on your career path? Did you always want to be a designer?

MN During my time at art school, having done painting and sculpture, I ended up in the jewellery department. I ended up thinking I was going to become a jeweller or a silversmith. The only reason I ended up in that department was because, within the art-school context, they were the only things that gave me a practical training of any kind. I discovered also that I had very little interest in jewellery or silversmithing. All I really wanted to know was how to make things.

In my last year or so I became interested in furniture – particularly chairs, which have become representative of design in a way not many other objects can be. I set about making furniture. That's how I started, as a kind of one-man operation physically making things and not really sure what I was going to do with them. One thing led to another and furniture evolved over the years into industrial design.

MF Talk us through the book.

MN What I have here is the first proof of the book, an unbound version. It's huge: 600 pages, very comprehensive, and I'd say 95 percent of

Name
Marc Newson
Occupation
Industrial designer
Location
His studio, London
Date
July 2012

the stuff I've done since the beginning of my career in 1984 is here. It spans almost 30 years, which is kind of terrifying. It goes right back to my days in art school, where I was already becoming preoccupied with watches and even strange pieces of furniture.

In 1986 I had my very first exhibition. It's interesting to point out, particularly in the context of the design-as-art phenomenon, I was designing furniture as sculpture at the beginning of my career. Not because I sensed there was any interest in those kinds of objects, but it's all I could do. I had to make these things as one-offs. I was literally making things myself. I was doing everything, from upholstery to machining to welding, you name it. The reason I did limited-edition pieces is not because I wanted them to be limited, necessarily, but because I couldn't make more than a certain number physically. Of course, when I got to the point where I was having exhibitions at the Gagosian Gallery, things changed. I was afforded a little more luxury in the ways I could work. So some of the work I've shown at the Gagosian is limited for other reasons.

There are chapters full of furniture to begin with. One of the first pieces, of course, was the Lockheed Lounge. There are these fantastic, funny anecdotal pieces in the book: there's the Vitra miniature of the Lockheed Lounge; there's a picture of Madonna with it in one of her videos; there's a fantastic film called Team America, where they used my Lockheed Lounge as a mini prop.

What's interesting is that I became known in the early days of my career as a furniture designer, but looking at my book it becomes evident to me that furniture represents a really small part of what I've done over the past 25 years.

The book shows the process from digital imagery, prototyping, choosing samples, approving the initial mouldings. There are lots of drawings throughout the book, hundreds of sketches, which are detailed very accurately. I've had a sketchbook with me by my side for the last 30 years.

There's all sorts of stuff in the book. Early works in carbon fibre, knives, a surfboard I made for a guy called Garrett McNamara. The board was actually shown at the Gagosian and sold as a piece of sculpture. Of course I've designed interiors, architecture, recording studios, restaurants, fashion boutiques and shop concepts for various people.

I've been working for the fashion brand G-Star for almost eight years. A lot of the garments have become cult garments; you will have seen celebrities wearing them at the MTV Awards. The G-Star Galaxy star-printed jacket was apparently very popular with Justin Bieber.

The airline Qantas has been one of my biggest clients. I've designed the aircraft interiors and all its airport lounges. The A380 aircraft interior was a big project I did for them, working very closely with Airbus. I've done lots of aeroplanes over the years, but the difference here is that I literally designed everything down to the cutlery. I also designed a range of luggage tags that contain RFI chips, so everyone knows where their luggage is at any moment. Qantas actually sells these to their passengers. No other airline in the world has luggage tags with RFI chips inside.

In the past ten years, designing things in the transport industry, particularly aviation, has accounted for 50 percent of the workload coming through my studio. It doesn't only include things like private jets, which I'm always designing – I've got two on the go right now. I started off doing cars. I designed a car for Ford back in 1999. All the analogue dials were controlled by a central toggle and operate electronically, like eyeballs. This was my idea, refining and distilling the controls you need to operate

'Chairs have become representative of design in a way not many other objects can be'

a car. I got it down to about eight things. I figured that's all you need to use a car. I don't really believe in using instruction manuals; I tend to throw them away.

One of the things that has preoccupied me over the years has been timepieces. I started a watch company called Ikepod back in 1994, but I started designing watches in 1986 – not only designed but built myself, so there are very intricate sketches in the book. The last piece I designed for Ikepod wasn't a watch. It was an hourglass, which was odd, because it wasn't particularly accurate but one of Ikepod's most successful products.

The most successful timepieces I designed were for the company Jaeger-LeCoultre. They're called Atmos clocks, large clocks that are almost self-perpetual; they're powered by small differences in temperature, so you never have to wind them. These were big, expensive objects but really fun, because working with people like Jaeger-LeCoultre, they're absolute experts in their field. I work with such a broad range of people. Some are great, some not so great, but these guys are great. They do what they do incredibly well, and for a designer that's always such a relief. You're not going to have to bang heads with people.

There's a huge section at the end of the book that I refer to as 'unreleased pieces'. These are concepts that were never realised or concepts that were manufactured in very limited quantities

but never made it through to production. Or in some cases just the studies that help me get from one place to another stylistically. I thought it would be interesting for people to see not only the real stuff that exists but the stuff that didn't, for one reason or another. One of the greatest projects that never happened was a series of optical products for a company called Swarovski Optik. I don't know if many people know that Swarovski makes the best binoculars and telescopes in the world for birdwatching and hunting. I designed a whole range of products for them.

    I think, all in all, this is one of the most comprehensive books on design I've ever seen. It's certainly the most comprehensive I'm ever going to do. It's huge and a bit unwieldy, but we just couldn't make it any thinner.

Above
The Ford 021C,
by Marc Newson

Neri Oxman

'In the digital revolution we're able to merge the intelligence of machines with the knowledge of craft'

Neri Oxman is an architect who founded the Mediated Matter research group at the MIT Media Lab. We spoke to her about her research into digital design and fabrication technologies, such as 3D printing.

Marcus Fairs What research have you been doing in 3D printing?

Neri Oxman I'm looking into the relationship between digital fabrication technologies at large, and 3D printing is one of those technologies that has been developing at a very rapid pace. But the way in which we design, the design process in relation to 3D printing, is still quite a traditional process. We design the form first, then we 3D-print it.

There are a lot of limitations with 3D printing. You can only use one material. And if you're using more than one material, you're still assigning those with specific geometries. You are defined by scale, which is the size of the printer. There are limitations to do with efficiency and limitations to do with time. We're looking into the natural world for inspiration, how to completely reinterpret or reinvent these digital fabrications. It's technology like 3D printing in the context of biology.

If you think about biological systems like human skin, for instance: in every pore in our body, we can find completely different skin properties. Our faces are made with skin that is relatively thin and with quite large pores and our back is made out of skin that is very thick with small pores. It's the same skin, only it acts as a filter in the face and as a barrier on the back. So depending on the performance, you're alternating material properties as a function of that structural environment.

How can we print that skin, or materials, that can respond to the natural environment with those continuous gradients? Given that all the natural systems we know are made of fibres, including human skin, we're now looking into fibre printing. What's nice about fibre printing is that you can control the density of the fibres, the articulations, the material's features, as a function of structural or environmental performance.

We started by looking at silkworms. Silkworms construct their cocoons using fibres and matrixes. Matrixes are the gooey materials that glue or bond the fibres together. What's so fascinating about the silkworm is that it creates the cocoon, which is this eggshell-like fibre, out of one continuous kilometre of silk. It's moving its head in an eight figure, in a motion that

Name
Neri Oxman
Occupation
Architect
Organisation
MIT
Location
MIT, Cambridge, via telephone
Date
January 2013

allows the silk to distribute itself, depending on the structural and environmental performance. For instance, the inner layers of the cocoon are soft and the outer layers of the cocoon are thick. The silkworm can vary the cocoon's properties according to the function.

What we've done is we've attached tiny magnets to the silkworms and we've managed to motion-track the movement of the silkworm as it's building its cocoon and translate the data to a 3D printer that's connected to a robotic arm. So just imagine that you have a regular 3D printer that's printing in X, Y and Z and now, because it's connected to a robotic arm, it can print in six axes instead of three. It has more degrees of freedom, so you're free-form printing. You're printing without support material. Like the silkworm, you're using the robotic arm to move freely in space, printing or depositing this material – which in our case is plastic or some other deposit material, which is deposited without any support materials.

In terms of the technological innovation, printing without support material is free-form printing. In terms of the design innovation, it's the ability to robotically weave those fibres through the use of 3D-printing technology. That's the part we're working on now.

The idea is to take any natural substance – in this case fibre-based materials, in another case cellular materials, like bone or tree – and translate the process of generating that geometry using 3D-printing technology. For instance, if you think about bone: bone varies its density in a cellular pattern. With that, the innovation was to create a 3D-printing platform that was able to continuously vary the density of the print. So whether it's a bone system or a tree or a silkworm, the precedents are implemented using a technology tool to help build more sustainable constructions but also, hopefully, build more beautiful ones.

MF What other materials are you printing with?

NO Concrete.

MF Using a robotic arm and six axes? It sounds like that's a major step forward from the usual way things are printed, when you have a gantry moving backwards and forwards. What could we be doing with this in, say, ten, 20, 30 years' time?

NO It's interesting because you can divide human civilisation into three chapters: before, during and after the Industrial Revolution. The digital age is where we live now. Before the Industrial Revolution we did everything by hand and that was when craft defined everything.

The most incredible examples of this craft are the ways the temples were built and the craftsman had this innate knowledge of how to vary the material according to the structural properties.

Neri Oxman

1 The Technion
Israel Institute
of Technology
is a university
in Haifa, Israel

The craftsman had that phenomenological knowledge about a material, much like a bird knows how to put more fibres together in order to keep the nest together. There is this material knowledge that has to do with craft that allowed us to build the Alhambra, or all those beautifully crafted sculptures that have remained intact for centuries.

Then came the Industrial Revolution and we started using the machine. The machine was used to standardise everything. And there is a standard for the machine, which in the case of

'We've managed to track the movement of the silkworm as it builds its cocoon and translate the data to a 3D printer connected to a robotic arm'

3D printing is the gantry. There's a standard for a window frame and there's a standard for a steel column. Everything we build is defined by these industrial standards. That's why all modern projects have this innate system that is inherent in the logic of buildings.

In the digital revolution, we're able to bring together the intelligence of the machine with the knowledge of craft. So craft meets the machine. I think what the robotic arm allows us to do today is to generate and control variation, on all scales: home, physical, architectural. We now have a moment where we can generate craft with the help of technology.

In the case of 3D printers, they have a gantry size that is limiting; three axes, which are limiting; support material, which is limiting. Once we fit the printer under a robotic arm, we free up all the limitations. The robotic arm uses a broom with za 20-metre reach, which controls not only the variation of properties like the cells of concrete but how we choose to assemble parts together.

In the bigger picture, I would see those three eras historically, and in the smaller picture, I would comment on 3D printing as a method for depositing material rather than a technology. Once you think about it in that way, you see it as a multi-agency of lots of tiny robots that are putting things together and printing something bigger.

MF In practical terms, how can this technology be used? Can it be used to construct entire buildings? Or would it just be used for façades or interior partitions?

NO I think both. We'll probably see more and more structural printing for façades and for building components that are not really structural. Once we figure out the scale limitations, once we move from the small robotic arm to a broom arm, then we'll be able to print a building. I think those things will go hand in hand, probably in the next decade. Definitely furniture and definitely products will be possible. But it will take quite a while before we are able to implement these technologies in the context of an entire building.

MF Can you tell us about yourself?

NO I was born in Israel. I'm half American, so I'm an American citizen. I went into the army, went into the air force and after that went to medical school, completed three years in medical school. I switched to architecture, went to the Technion[1] for my first three years, then went to the Architectural Association in London for my diploma. Then I went to work for Kohn Pedersen Fox in Covent Garden in London, which I miss so much. After that I went to do a PhD in the computation group in the Department of Architecture at MIT, and after completing the PhD I enrolled in the faculty of the MIT Media Lab, where I started the media and arts research.

MF So you're working across different disciplines, not just in architecture.

NO That's absolutely right.

Kieran Long

'Design is more interesting when it's about how we live together than what we buy for our homes'

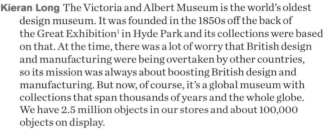

The senior curator of contemporary architecture, design and digital at London's V&A Museum discussed the controversial acquisition of the world's first 3D-printed gun.

Marcus Fairs What is the V&A?

Kieran Long The Victoria and Albert Museum is the world's oldest design museum. It was founded in the 1850s off the back of the Great Exhibition[1] in Hyde Park and its collections were based on that. At the time, there was a lot of worry that British design and manufacturing were being overtaken by other countries, so its mission was always about boosting British design and manufacturing. But now, of course, it's a global museum with collections that span thousands of years and the whole globe. We have 2.5 million objects in our stores and about 100,000 objects on display.

Name
Kieran Long
Occupation
Curator
Organisation
V&A Museum
Location
V&A Museum,
London
Date
September 2013

MF We're here during the London Design Festival. What do you think is London's position in the design world today?

KL I think it's the most competitive, the most thrilling city in the world. The V&A was invented at a moment when Britain was the world's manufactory. It's certainly no longer that, but London, as a city, is a kind of brain trust of the world. Working in a place like the V&A feels like the most incredible crossroads of intellectuals, designers and creatives.

MF Why is that?

KL I think London has always been a place that's incredibly tolerant of new things, of people arriving in the city. We know that the city is based on immigration, it's based on people who are already here tolerating them and we're really comfortable with that. I think there are threats to that. Certainly we should keep London as open as it can be. Any political agenda that's about closing that down somehow is, to me, anathema to what London really is. In terms of design and architecture, we have some of the greatest schools in the world. A lot of people study here.

MF Is one of the big threats not allowing foreign students access to London universities?

KL I think any kind of political agenda that tries to limit the influx of international students to the UK is a disaster for the schools and a disaster for the design culture here – because, let's face it, if those people weren't coming and designing here, there's no manufacturing. What we are is a crossroads for great creative people to come and learn from their peers, to start new things and

then go back, with those things, to the countries they come from. Or to come here and make London a richer place. Anything that stops that would be a disaster.

MF One of the items on show in the New Acquisitions Gallery is a 3D-printed gun. Why did the V&A acquire something like this?

KL We've got five new acquisitions in this gallery that are backed by the Design Fund – an amazing fund dedicated to contemporary acquisitions for the collection. Most exciting for me, because it's something that I and my colleague Louise Shannon have been working on, is the acquisition of this 3D-printed gun, designed by Cody Wilson of Defense Distributed in Texas. It is the first functioning gun that could be 3D-printed anywhere in the world. You need to add a metal nail as the firing pin, but you could

Above
The Liberator 3D-printed gun by Cody Wilson of Defense Distributed

1 The Great
Exhibition of the
Works of Industry
of all Nations was
held in London's
Hyde Park in 1851

theoretically 3D-print every other component and shoot someone, if you can get some ammunition.

It has caused a lot of fuss in the press, that the V&A would acquire an object like this. But what I've been pleased about is that people have seen it not as something that is deliberately shocking, but as a good signpost for where manufacturing might be going and the implications of new technology.

Something I'm really passionate about is showing the political backgrounds of things, even when they might not be palatable. I don't believe that everyone should be carrying guns

'The 3D-printed gun and its distribution online are acts of politics as much as acts of design'

and that's not what we're advocating here. What we are saying is that this is possible and we might have to do something about it if we don't want something like this to happen. Design, for me, is the thing that really focuses those questions. When you see those things for real, it's different to reading about them on the internet. You think, 'Can all those things really go together and kill someone?' And the answer is yes.

MF 3D printing has been around for a long time and guns have been around for a long time, so why is this object important?

KL There's a lot of technocratic optimism around 3D printing, particularly in the design world. People say it's going to be great. You'll be able to print out your kids' toys, fix the hook on the back of the bathroom door, those kinds of things. But when Cody Wilson released this, I think it transformed that conversation. It changed it into one about ethical issues, about how we want to live together, how new technologies affect our relationships to one another.

MF How did you acquire the gun? Was it very difficult getting it through customs?

KL My colleague Louise Shannon flew to Austin and visited Cody Wilson in his workshop. It's a room about the size of a toilet with a 3D printer in one corner and him on his laptop in the other. That's it. Now we're working very hard to get those objects into the UK.

The fun thing about the V&A is that we have a collection of arms and armour, we have guns in the collection. There's nothing strange about that, and actually we have all the licences to import firearms. And Cody Wilson himself is a licensed weapon

100

manufacturer in the US. The only problem we've had has been getting an export licence for him.

MF So this isn't actually a gun he printed?

KL The one we have on display right now is actually a stand-in. We printed that out here in London. The prototypes that Cody is sending us are currently sitting in an airport waiting to get on a plane as soon as the relevant licence is given. In a way, this gun printed here in London becomes part of the story of the difficulty of getting it into the UK.

MF What were Wilson's motivations for printing a gun? Was it to prove a point? Was it to raise an ethical dilemma?

KL He's incredibly articulate with his reasons for doing this. One of the things I love that he says is that this is not about design; this is a political act. That's what he calls it. He believes firmly that the United States Constitution guarantees that everyone has a right to bear arms. The design of the gun and its distribution online are acts of politics as much as they are acts of design.

MF What is your definition of design?

KL My guiding principle here at the museum is that design is more interesting when it's about how we live together than when it's about what we buy for our homes. The V&A might very well be seen as a place of bourgeois objects that end up in grand houses. Historically we've collected a lot of that stuff and we will continue to do so, but my passion is for objects that tell you something about the public realm. When you walk down the street, how is your relationship with your fellow man changed with something like a 3D-printed gun in the world?

Barber & Osgerby

'They very generously gave us ten days to design the Olympic Torch'

Speaking to us just before the 2012 Olympic Games in London, the founders of industrial design studio Barber&Osgerby explained the evolution of their design for the Olympic Torch.

Ben Hobson How did you come to design the Olympic Torch?

Ed Barber It was 2010 when we won an international competition to do the torch. LOCOG[1] very generously gave us ten days to design it.

BH What was it about your design that won over the judges?

EB There are two very distinctive parts of the design of the torch. One is that it's triangular, and that relates to the fact that the Olympic Games have been in London three times.

Jay Osgerby In addition, the torch has an array of 8000 perforations, or circles. The 8000 perforations symbolise the 8000 people who carry the torch. And as well as symbolising the 8000 torch bearers, it symbolises the 8000 miles the torch will travel.

BH Do the holes have a practical use, or are they just decorative?

JO All the holes help to dissipate the heat. The top of the torch has a flame that gets to 700 degrees centigrade, but because of the way the holes are arrayed around it, the heat dissipates before it gets to the handle. So we could use one material in the torch without having to transfer to an insulating material for the handle.

Names
Ed Barber and
Jay Osgerby
Occupation
Industrial
designers
Company
Barber&Osgerby
Location
Vitra showroom,
London
Date
May 2012

EB The other reason for the holes is that it gives a very good grip. In the briefing document was a chart of different weather conditions, and there was a lot of mention of snow, rain and high wind speed, so we thought a good grip was essential. The torch bearers included lots of children, and a woman who's apparently 100.

JO We wanted to make something that didn't feel like a trophy you put on the mantelpiece, rather something that felt part of the Games, that fell more into sporting equipment, less ceremonial.

EB [Tapping the display case] I hope this case is nice and secure because apparently they're going for a bit on eBay at the moment.

BH How is the torch constructed?

JO It's two layers of laser-cut aluminium. And at the top and bottom you have two aluminium die castings that are welded together, so the whole assembly becomes a monocoque structure – very strong, light and tensile, so it does something other than just look nice.

1 LOCOG was
the London
Organising
Committee of
the 2012 Olympic
and Paralympic
Games

The other thing the perforations enable is a view through, because we thought it would be pretty cool to see the inner workings. So much effort has gone into creating the burner, we thought it would be interesting to see the canister and the burner suspended within the mesh of the two skins. Also, the flames don't just come out the top, they also come out the side. We like the idea that it accentuated the movement.

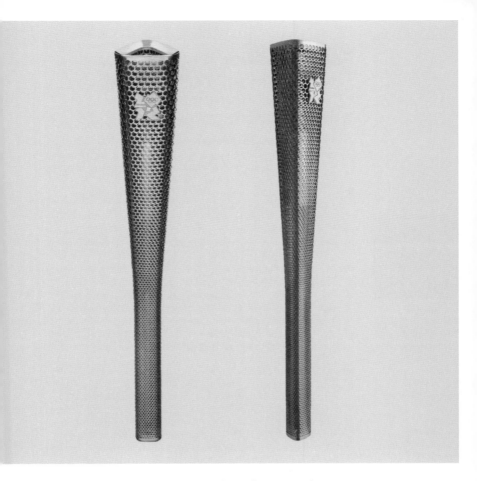

It also helps with what's called the kiss, when two torches come together. It's important that the burner itself is preheated by the previous torch, because it helps to evaporate the gas from the canister. When you put the two torches together, the flame from one doesn't only ignite the gas but it also preheats the burner assembly. The holes help that, enabling the heat to go into the top.

BH How can you know it will function well out on the road? Have you done performance tests?

EB The torch has been very well tested. It has been to a BMW wind tunnel in Munich, in torrential rain, snow, all kinds of weather. Fingers crossed, we shouldn't have too many what are called flameouts. Every torch relay has flameouts, but we're aiming to have the least number of those.

Above
The 2012 Olympic
Torch by
Barber & Osgerby

Peter Zumthor
'There's something beautiful about an enclosed garden – a degree of intimacy'

Peter Zumthor's 2011 Serpentine Gallery Pavilion was as much about the garden at its centre as the structure that surrounded it. The Swiss architect discussed his relationship with gardens and why he isn't in architecture for the glory.

Marcus Fairs I'm sure I'm going to ask you the same things everyone else has asked you.

Peter Zumthor Try to ask something different.

MF You know what, if you want to just say something different in response to my questions, just do that. Tell me the story that you want to tell.

PZ My name is Peter Zumthor, 'Zumthor' meaning 'by the gate'. A nice name for an architect, I think. I grew up in the city of Basel, in Switzerland. I learned first a profession as a cabinetmaker, then I went to art school. Then slowly, slowly I fought to be an architect and I think architecture is a beautiful profession. I am a passionate architect. I am not going for commercial projects. I go for projects that I can put my heart into and projects which I think are worth doing.

MF How did that philosophy lead you here to the Serpentine?

PZ I did this project because gardens have become more and more important for me working as an architect. The process at the beginning was more about seeing landscape and gardens from the outside, but the longer I work, the more I want them to be inside. Maybe I would even like to be submerged within the gardens. I have done a couple of projects along these lines – and this is now one of them – where I make a building that acts as a frame, as a stage for a garden. The garden is in the centre: not you, not me and not anyone else. We are around the garden and not the other way around.

Many of us know, have some vague knowledge, that an enclosed garden, there's something beautiful about it, a degree of intimacy. It's these plants. It's the sky. It's the birds. As we told people to be quiet for the interview, you can see how beautiful it becomes. That is how it should be.

I asked Piet Oudolf, the garden designer, to 'paint' the garden and he did a marvellous job. There was no discussion. I trusted him. And he surprised me with this wonderful garden with a lot of beautiful flowers, the kind you would find on the edge of a field. There is a statement here, I think. Or maybe there's no statement. This depends.

Name
Peter Zumthor
Occupation
Architect
Location
Serpentine Gallery Pavilion, London
Date
June 2011

MF Can you tell us about the architectural concept?

PZ This garden is a typological piece, it's a type. It's not a contextual piece. So in a way, this kind of viewing device can be anywhere. It is a more eternal piece. You can put it up somewhere else, it would have other plants and another sky and another climate. So let's see what happens to this. I think the chances are good that it will be put up again and I will see then what's in it.

MF Are you as interested in gardens as you are in architecture?

PZ When I was young, I was looking at the gardens outside. I enjoyed them but not really consciously. And the older I get, the interest becomes more keen. My work reflects this desire to know more about the garden, to integrate the garden, or maybe even make the garden the centrepiece and the architecture just a frame.

Above
The 2011
Serpentine
Gallery
Pavilion by
Peter Zumthor

Tom Dixon

'I've had an accidental career. I hope more accidents happen, because they're always fortuitous'

As part of a series of chat shows at Design Miami 2008, we spoke to British designer Tom Dixon about his flame-cut steel furniture and how music and motorbikes impacted on his design career.

Marcus Fairs Would you say that you define yourself as a British designer?

Name
Tom Dixon
Occupation
Industrial designer
Location
Design Miami, Miami
Date
December 2008

Tom Dixon When I looked through the lineup of speakers today, it was good to see that our national identity, despite globalisation, is still present. Because I'm totally defined by my parents, by my English father and my mother, who's half-French, and my Latvian grandfather. I was born in Tunisia and I've lived in both Egypt and Morocco as well. I'm a European, even though I pretend to be British, because it's easier to be sometimes, but I'm actually a European. Like I say, despite us all travelling to the same places, listening to the same music, reading the same magazines and watching the same films, we're still very different, which is ultimately what design does. It tries to create a difference from what is there already or what is going to happen next.

MF So you identify yourself as a European. Yet your early work was very much based in a particular time and place in London, during a major recession. Would you say you were influenced by that?

TD When I was maturing, when I was at school, London was depressing but it was also fabulous because there was a lot of freedom. It was a very cheap place to live, which it isn't now. I didn't dream of being a designer, like everybody seems to want to be now. I had normal dreams of being in the music business. When you're young in London, you have to have a band, right? What's good about being in a band is that it teaches you to create your own product, to learn your own instrument, to learn your own songs. You have your own gigs and print your own posters.

My experience in music was something that I transferred to the design business later on. The bass guitar was my liberation. I was a very shy boy and being in a band made you more popular. I still have a guitar that was actually an old Sex Pistols instrument. I bought it off a roadie, and for me that guitar is a symbol of freedom, really. It got me out and about and creating, so I initially wanted to be a musician.

MF Why are you a designer, rather than a musician, today?

TD I had a motorbike accident, which stopped me doing any of that. And I broke my leg. I've had a very accidental career, is what I'm getting at. I hope more accidents happen because they've always been fortuitous. Things that look bad often turn out to be really good.

The motorbike itself is a symbol of liberty and freedom and also productivity in London – it's not quite as big as São Paulo but it's definitely eight million people. You can't do anything in London without a motorcycle, so I reckon I'm probably twice as productive as non-motorcycling designers.

I still ride every day despite having had several accidents. I had an accident in Milan. I had a scooter and I'm used to riding motorbikes and it's got different controls. They ride on the wrong side of the road. I just went too far around the corner from the scooter shop, but I got a lot of sympathy for it and it gave me something to talk about in interviews. I didn't break my knee but it was kind of nasty.

MF You have some work here at Design Miami from your Flame series. Tell us about this project.

TD Well, I've been walking around Design Miami for two years now and I've always wondered, 'How can I be more extravagant, more gilded, more floral, more polished than all the designers in there?' And I've realised, I just can't. So this Flame chair is kind of 'anti'. It's a very rough thing, very heavy. It was originally created for Sudeley Castle in Oxfordshire, which goes back to the fourteenth century, which had seen a lot of destruction during the English Civil War. All the contents were destroyed, so this was an attempt at permanence as well. What's good about this chair is that it will last and it will come back to Sudeley Castle in Oxfordshire, which is still there despite having been nearly destroyed in the seventeenth century. It's still an active place. So there's a positive message.

MF The pieces in the Flame collection are extremely heavy, made from steel nearly four centimetres thick, which has been cut with a flame cutter, I guess?

TD Yes, and the pieces are going to mature for a couple of years after having a bit of rust growing on them.

My theory is that design doesn't really exist. It's something you apply to the other trades. But the expression of the Flame furniture really is fantastic, thick steel that people use. It's great this season that, because of the recession, steel has gone down from £300 per tonne to £45 per tonne, so it's more affordable.

MF You seem to really enjoy working with metal.

TD There's something quite nice about the industrial nature of metal, but also the manual nature of it. There's that balance and the love, the handiwork. I love industry as well. Welding was a revelation to me and the idea of putting things together very quickly, putting them together and taking them apart to make something new, is a method well suited to my very short attention span.

I'm very lucky. Most people don't get a chance to make something, finish it off and maybe even sell it in a single day. It doesn't happen any more, unless you're a baker.

I've got that opportunity, but I've got the opportunity of working with bigger industry as well and having things that go all over the world. I might be turning up somewhere like Korea or Vietnam and I might see my lamp somewhere in somebody's home or shop. It's great to have a passport to lots of different companies.

MF Do you have a standard method of working? For instance, do you start by sketching or do you just go and grab some material and begin sculpting?

TD I tend to avoid working, really. I've perfected the technique of being naïve about stuff and maintaining a distance from being an expert. I mean, there are a lot of experts here today, but for me personally, I'm always better when I don't know anything about the subject I'm working with, so I can approach it completely fresh and not have any preconceptions. That's a really hard thing to expect, being idiotic about stuff and being able to see it as a baby might. But that's my method – it's to try to not know much about stuff.

MF You started out making handmade objects or repurposing found items, and I remember talking to you a couple of years ago and you said there wasn't much demand for it.

TD There still isn't.

MF You went into another kind of industrial design. But then you realised that shows like Design Miami elevated the concept of the handmade piece and you started doing that again.

TD These things are cyclical. But there's definitely something nice about the opportunity here in Miami, not only to create individual things but to participate in this expensive experiment. It's rather difficult to do. What's fantastic about Design Miami is that it gives you enough space to be able to explain things. And, if you're lucky, you'll make enough cash to indulge in some of your fantasies.

I'm hoping that it will also provide me with the opportunity to push the design conversation further, because you do tend to see some interesting stuff that way. I've just walked out of the design showroom Luminaire, where there's a fantastic project with 100 paper sculptors talking about cancer. I think those kinds of things will become more important.

I think designers need to take themselves beyond the bling and into some much more serious subjects. I know I'm part of the

problem, but I'm hoping the platform exists to make a bigger impact. I think designers can be quite powerful, linked up with industry and finance and distribution. For too long we've been too introverted and too self-satisfied. So I think there are more important things to do now.

Iris van Herpen
'Everybody could have their body scanned and order clothes that fit perfectly'

The Dutch fashion designer pioneered the use of 3D printing to create spectacular haute couture collections. She spoke to us about the future of 3D printing and how it could one day transform our clothes.

Claire Barrett What was it about 3D printing that first got you interested in it?

Iris van Herpen With 3D printing, it was the first time I could translate the 3D image I had in my mind immediately to the 3D model in the computer and then the 3D printer. With handwork or with the usual method of fashion designing, I have something in my head that's three-dimensional, which first has to be translated into something two-dimensional, like a drawing, then it goes back to three dimensionality again, so it feels really old-school. It's a strange way of working – you have a step in between.

Name
Iris van Herpen
Occupation
Fashion designer
Location
Amsterdam,
via telephone
Date
January 2013

The things I have 3D printed I could never have done by hand. It would have just been impossible. The beauty of handwork is that it's always a bit different and you can never create something totally symmetrical. At the same time, I think that's the beauty of 3D printing – it is 100 percent symmetrical in the smallest details, even the printing layers. And that's the fingerprint of the technique.

CB Was the use of digital technology something you were exposed to in college?

IvH No, it's actually really funny. When I was young I was raised without television and we didn't have a computer. I think we were the last people to have the internet and when I was at college I didn't have a computer. I actually took computer lessons but I didn't like the computer at all.

I had discussions with my computer teacher and he told me, 'You just can't work without a computer,' and then I became really stubborn and I thought, 'I can. Just watch me.' I did everything by hand, all the time. But being exposed to 3D printing, I suddenly saw how many possibilities it would give me in terms of three dimensionality, which convinced me to start working with technology.

CB Did your collaborations start from wanting to work in a more digital way?

IvH It's definitely unusual for a fashion designer to collaborate with scientists and architects. But with my 3D-printing work

I always collaborate with an architect or someone who specialises in 3D modelling because I don't specialise in it myself. I know a little bit about it, but not nearly as much as the people who work with me. If you're starting from scratch using a technique that someone else is already very experienced in, I think that's a waste of time.

Even if it hadn't been necessary, I would have still done it that way because I don't want to walk in circles, like being in my own mind all the time. For this collection, for example, we worked with the architects Neri Oxman, Julia Koerner and Philip Beesley. We've really been bringing two worlds together, because I think fashion is super-interesting but the architects are just as important to me.

Above
A 3D-printed garment from the 2010 Crystallization collection by Iris van Herpen with .MGX by Materialise and designer Daniel Widrig

Iris van Herpen

IvH I'm really open to sharing ideas and working with somebody, but I feel like fashion is quite a locked industry. The technology is there but the fashion industry is not ready for 3D printing. Fashion designers are used to collaborating but usually with the musicians they dress, or an artist who makes a print for them. Working with scientists, architects or people who have different knowledge is just not a part of fashion, and that's something that surprises me.

CB Are you interested in developing new materials yourself?

IvH I'm always getting inspired by new materials, but I feel like I'm just choosing them at the moment, not designing them. It takes a long time to design a material, so you can't do it for every

'The things I've 3D printed I could never have done by hand. It would have just been impossible'

season. But if you're able to create something new at least every one or two years, I think that gives you more control over your design process.

CB Your early 3D-printed pieces were like sculpture or body armour. Are the latest ones more wearable?

IvH They're definitely more wearable. I'm really happy that my 3D prints are finally acting with the movements of the body. These days a girl can even dance in them. The 2013 Voltage collection was really a big step forward because it was totally flexible and the jacket we created, for example, you could even put it in the washing machine. You could sit on it. It's really a regular garment now.

With the Voltage collection I really tried to make the clothes step away from the realm of sculpture and find their own field in between traditional woven fabrics and 3D-printed fabrics. With 3D printing you can decide how much flexibility you want on a specific part, like the knees or the shoulders, in millimetres or centimetres. And you can just include those measurements on the file. Also, you can include colours in the 3D prints. The colouring is in the file; it's not something you add later on. That's been a big step. If we continue with that, we'll be able to create 2D prints within the 3D prints and then it'll feel like we're creating something in 4D.

CB How long do you think it will be before 3D-printed clothing becomes mainstream?

IvH I would love to be the first to include 3D printing in ready-to-wear. The flexibility is there. I think now the focus is on developing the materials, the long-term quality and the size, because there are no printers that can print a whole dress yet.

But fashion is a big industry. You have all the factories with the traditional sewing machines, so I can imagine the industry will not be ready for such a big change because you need technical people with knowledge of 3D printing, 3D printers and software, instead of people who know how to sew a seam.

CB Can you foresee a time when people will be able to download and print out an Iris van Herpen dress at home?

IvH Of course. I can actually imagine everybody having their own 3D skin and being able to just order something online. But I don't know if people will print it out at home. I can imagine you could have printing factories, order your dress and maybe the customer gets a little bit of a say in it as well. They could say, 'Well, I want this one but with longer sleeves.'

Everybody could have their body scanned and order clothes that fit perfectly. I think it's old-fashioned that only the 100 richest women in the world have clothes that actually fit them and I think 3D printing can really fill a gap there.

Oki Sato

'A good idea is something you can tell your mother on the phone. If she thinks it's interesting, it's good'

The founder of Japanese design studio Nendo talked about the store he designed in New York for shoe brand Camper, the importance of telling stories through design and the poor quality of his sketches.

Marcus Fairs We're in Camper's new store in New York, surrounded by white plastic shoes. What was the idea behind your design?

Oki Sato I'd been working with Camper for a few years on their small retail stores when they asked me to find a solution for their big stores with really high ceilings. Obviously the product is really small, and they didn't know how to use the ceiling height. They had been using a lot of graphics on the ceiling, but it looked really empty.

What I did was fill the walls with these plastic shoes. Most of them are fake, so you have to find the real shoes among them. What it does is make the products, forms and colours stand out in the space and create a contrast. In terms of acoustics, it absorbs sound, so it feels much more comfortable. It starts with a single product, but by copying and pasting it becomes an interior element. It catches light and shadow and gives texture to the space.

Name
Oki Sato
Occupation
Designer
Company
Nendo
Location
Camper store,
New York
Date
May 2013

MF Will you be doing more stores like this?

OS We designed another one in Madrid. The Madrid store has a lot of windows, so it really reacts to the natural light.

MF You work on an incredibly wide range of projects.

OS I enjoy designing anything, whether it's a paperclip or a big interior. It's all basically the same for me. I'm just addicted to design and I enjoy what I'm doing.

MF What is your design process? How do you start?

OS The process is fairly basic. I start from rough sketches. I'm not a good sketcher; I do stupid sketches. But then we move onto renderings and models; we make a lot of models. We have three rapid prototyping machines in our studio, which work 24 hours a day because it's really important to see the form physically.

It's really the story that is the important thing for me. When I meet a new client, I hear what's going on and if I cannot come up with a nice story or solution for them, it's difficult for me.

MF Is drawing still the most important way to express ideas?

OS I have a feeling that when you're a good sketcher, it makes the story a bit blurry. Since I'm not good at sketching, it helps me. But it has to be something everyone can understand. A good idea has to be something you can tell your mother or a small child about on the phone. If she thinks it's interesting, then it's good design.

MF What is design to you?

OS Design is emotional. It's about how people feel when they approach a design. It's about making a connection between objects or space and people. It shouldn't be centre stage; it should support people.

MF Does the work you do vary according to the country or region?

OS We do a lot of interiors in Asia and a lot of furniture in Europe. But I think Dezeen took away all the boundaries between countries and cultures. Everyone knows everything now. If there's something interesting in Dezeen, the next month all the students will be doing something similar. I think that's amazing.

MF Camper said people were coming into the store today because they saw the story we published yesterday.

OS That's the Dezeen effect!

Above
Nendo's Camper
store on Fifth
Avenue, New York

Tim Kobe
'The Apple Store wasn't right by conventional retail wisdom. But it was right for Apple'

The co-founder of strategic design firm Eight Inc talked about what it was like working with Steve Jobs on Apple's first store and his view that women are the biggest new emerging market.

Marcus Fairs What is Eight Inc and what do you do?

Tim Kobe We have eight offices globally: four in Asia, three in the US and one in the UK. I'm the CEO and founder of Eight and I'm now based in Singapore.

We're trained as architects, communication designers and industrial designers but our focus is really on creating the best possible experience for the user. So whether that's architectural or whether that's branding and retail, what someone experiences within an environment is something we've been focused on for many years. And it's helped distinguish us from our peers.

MF Who have you worked with over the years?

TK We've worked for 14 or 15 years with Apple. We've worked with Virgin, Coach and Citibank and we've worked in automotive and hospitality industries. I think we have a unique approach to understanding brands and the experience people have with them, so a lot of our larger corporate clients tend to keep us for many years. And we evolve that experience as the brand moves forward and its values evolve and change.

MF Why did you relocate from San Francisco to Singapore?

TK I started the company in San Francisco, but after many years, our core US and European clients began pushing us to have more presence in Asia. And so, as a result of pressure from clients and the new opportunities we had, it made sense for us to come here and grow into the Asian market. What we've found is there's an incredible opportunity for what we do – both as a bridge from existing brands and mature markets and for brands that are competitive in Asian markets. In China, for example. Many brands now are wanting to grow into globally recognised companies.

MF Why Singapore?

TK There's a natural vibrancy to Singapore. Of course for starting a business, they have an amazing system here. But when you look at it from a regional market standpoint, we can be in Beijing, India or Australia in six or eight hours. We really have a broad reach from Singapore.

MF What is the Asian market for design services?

TK The markets change, so it's hard to lump together Asia as one market. If you look at maturity in China compared to Indonesia or

Name
Tim Kobe
Occupation
Designer
Company
Eight Inc
Location
Inside
Festival,
Singapore
Date
October 2013

Australia, they are really radically different. For us, it's more complex in terms of understanding the cultural nuances. But I think people are recognising that there is incredible value in creating relevant design work and they recognise that there's a competitive advantage in it. So from a business and branding perspective, that's something more and more people are appreciating here.

MF Do you think this part of the world is leaving the West behind? Is it innovating in terms of design?

TK I wouldn't say that Asia is leaving the West behind; it's coming into its own. I think Asians are starting to create their own identity, to recognise that they have distinctive qualities and conditions that can add to the global design conversation. I think there are distinctive characteristics that the different markets possess, and they're continuing to develop.

MF What about China?

TK We've been talking with officials from the Chinese government and they told us that Europe has 94 globally recognised brands, the US has 91 and China has three. There's a lot of concern, as things are changing exponentially, about China's ability to develop its own brands. Business has primarily been focused internally, so you have two brands in the same category competing with each other, but within the Chinese market. They don't necessarily resonate with an international market, and it's something the Chinese are very concerned about.

There's an extreme sense of urgency for China because labour is becoming less competitive, they are investing heavily in Africa and other places where they have labour resources as well as physical resources and they don't possess brands that are competitive. If Europe has Airbus and the US has Boeing, what do the Chinese have in the airline category? You can go from there down to drink brands and watches or what have you.

MF So the Chinese are talking to you because they want you to help them build something?

TK I think that's what they're asking. What are the right solutions? On one hand, the easiest thing is to go out and purchase a company and take that installed knowledge, just occupy that shell. But they're also interested in creating new brands that make their society more than just a consumption society. As manufacturing continues to move away from China, the Chinese don't want to be experiencing some of the things the US may be experiencing today, with much of the manufacturing and production gone offshore. It has to do with fundamental aspects of the structural stability of the company.

MF How did your work with Apple come about?

TK We were brought in as one of Apple's major outside consultants when Steve Jobs first came back to the company. We started doing

Tim Kobe

launches, product introductions and conferences, so we were already working on the brand experience for Apple. Then I wrote a paper on retail and gave it to Steve. He called us one day and said, 'Hey, I want you guys to come in and start thinking about retail.'

We started with a blank whiteboard, drawing bubbles on the wall. The programme was really a collaborative effort. There were a lot of people coming and going in terms of evolving it, building mock-ups and exploring different things. Communication and environmental designers were in that process, people dealing with the behaviour of the staff, the products and services. It all had to work together so that there was a seamless experience with the Apple brand.

MF Let's talk about the first Apple Store on Fifth Avenue in New York. Why was that Apple Store different?

TK In the very beginning, Apple had four products: two desktop computers and two laptops. Steve wanted a 6000-square-foot space, so there were many things we had to bring into that space besides presentation of the product. There were a lot of experiential kinds of things – solution-based experiences, a kids' area that targeted certain markets, the Genius Bar, the theatre. Many aspects of the overall design were unique to the Apple brand.

The Fifth Avenue store, if we look at the conventional rules of retail, would violate the usual checklist. It's in a basement, there's no product display in the window. It's three streets off the primary shopping street in New York City – or at least it used to be. It wasn't right by conventional retail wisdom but it was right for Apple. That's what made it distinctive. I think it was about recognising the core brand values of the company and delivering an experience that's aligned with that. If you can make emotional connections between the brand and the customer, all these pieces add up to something more compelling.

MF Why did Apple decide it needed to sell its products in its own branded stores?

TK If you look at where Apple used to sell: it had an online presence and a retail channel presence. That meant that if you were in a store, you had to express your brand in the same way everyone talked about brands. People would come in and say, 'Hey, I'm interested in an Apple computer – this speed, this price.' And the salesperson might say, 'This brand has the same features as Apple but it's cheaper.' So people were typically counterselling against Apple. And when you let that channel define the game, in terms of presenting your brand, you're at a disadvantage.

So for Apple to step out, redefine itself and really express its brand value through that experience, that's going to hand them the opportunity to separate. And once that happened, the traditional third-party channels were beating a path to their door. But it was really about controlling the message and drawing on the customer experience.

MF Was Steve Jobs heavily involved in the store design?

TK Steve hadn't had a great experience in retail when we started the programme. What he did have was an intuitive sense of what Apple's brand qualities were and how they could be applied. When we tried dense presentations of the product, it didn't feel like Apple. It wasn't open enough, it wasn't accessible, democratic or simple enough. Once we could create more space, simplify the offering, make a more natural ease of use – those were all characteristics that had been part of the Apple brand since the beginning. Steve was really instrumental in making sure we were delivering that experience, strategically on brand with the Apple qualities.

MF You've mentioned that Steve was nervous the night before the first opening.

TK It was a little disconcerting. We had just finished the first store, working all night and setting up all the product and the lighting and adjusting everything. Steve was sitting on one of the tables and we were all just standing around. And he said, 'Guys, what happens if nobody comes tomorrow?' And we all sort of went, 'That can't be possible.' But he was recognising that there were a lot of critics out there at the time.

It wasn't without a certain degree of risk, and it was visible. At that time Apple had two percent market share. He wasn't 100 percent convinced that it would be as successful as it became. That's something that speaks to his character and vision – that he would take that risk. And from the first year it opened, we

'You have to reinvent retail every five years. If you're not reinventing it, you're losing your advantage'

started evolving the design. It started to change and continue to evolve. Learning from experience with people and retail, it was something we could continue to refine and make better.

MF You also said in your talk that with retail you can't stay still – you need to reinvent every five years. You said that since Steve died, the pace of change at Apple has slowed a bit.

TK Yes, I think when you look at retail you have to reinvent every five years. If you're not reinventing it, you're losing your advantage. Steve was always very driven at staying an arm's length ahead of everyone else. And I think many competitors have made rapid changes to either emulate aspects of the Apple Store or to have a much bigger presence. I think the design is getting a little long in the tooth, in terms of continuing to roll out the same type of solution. So my sense is that retail is a competitive environment, and I think Apple's ready for that next shift.

MF What do you think the next emerging market is, the next shift?

TK It's not China, it's not Brazil, it's not India, it's not Indonesia. It's actually women. Globally, women are probably the greatest growth opportunity. One of the things we've seen with the companies we work with is that, traditionally, there's been this functional brand ideal and, to a large degree, that's really targeted toward a male sensibility and male behaviour. But

'The next emerging market is not China, it's not Brazil, it's not India and it's not Indonesia. It's actually women'

women are becoming more influential in the marketplace – I think 62 percent or 65 percent of business school graduates in the US are female today. So hotels, airlines and retail have to shift towards more of an emotional brand ideal versus the functional brand ideal.

I think we're going to see a lot more work in that area, where people are actually focusing on the female customer and delivering an experience that's actually better for everyone. Because women tend to have a different set of sensibilities and I think it's going to change all those categories.

MF Have you got any concrete examples of what that means for store designers and product designers? Have you got any work that is targeted at women?

TK One of our clients, a large hospitality client, has looked at this condition and started to think about the aspects of hospitality design that will fundamentally shift to be more successful for female customers. If you look at the way most hotels have been set up, for male business travellers, there's the typical location, the typical bars – the fundamentals of the experience are there to cater to the male business traveller.

When that becomes a female business traveller, the ways you interact with them, the kinds of experiences they're looking for, the issues with sanitation – all these components have to be considered differently and that's changing the way people think about creating a new type of experience.

MF Will that change the entire landscape of design? From products to spaces, will things look different?

TK I think they will. When we start to explore what might be more relevant for female customers, I think the engagement will start to shift. Our experience in retail helps us to understand, as we do a lot of retail that's targeted toward women. But if you look at hospitality and airline travel, when you look at a lot of the considerations of the female audience, the shifts in behaviour, products and services will naturally have to follow suit.

Rem Koolhaas
'It's a cliché that everyone is living in the city. We're thinking in new ways about the countryside'

We were invited to look around OMA's De Rotterdam building, where Dutch architect Rem Koolhaas talked about shifting his focus from urbanism to the countryside, despite just having completed another skyscraper.

Amy Frearson What did you set out to achieve with the design of De Rotterdam?

Rem Koolhaas It's a building that we started in the late 1990s for a developer. We all know that these days cities and states don't have deep pockets, so from the beginning it was a building that was defined to a large extent by financial considerations. The developer wanted to combine offices, housing, a hotel and other facilities. They never were quite sure in what proportion, so we made a building of separate volumes that were slightly shifted vis-a vis one another, so it was very adaptable. We could easily replace one part with another part and therefore accommodate different kinds of logics and arguments.

This shifting creates a large building, but a large building that is a dynamic presence in the city. It's very different from any angle. It can be a wall. It can be almost three separate buildings. It can be a single mass. That became the main ambition: a building that really creates maximum benefit from its situation. It is on the other side of the river and can only be approached by one bridge, so we could easily predict how it would be perceived and that is very rare. That is what we made the source of our effort.

AF You've said in the past that the brief was for two buildings.

RK It was actually two separate sides, and after a while we discovered it was smarter to combine it in a single structure, because then you could be more flexible and make changes more easily. I also like the urban effect of this building more than simply planting needles on this very large part of the harbour.

AF Would you say the building is reflective of OMA's current approach to buildings?

RK I don't think so. We design many tall buildings but this is only the third or fourth of our realisations. One is in London, on a site where we're certain nobody will actually see the entire building. De Rotterdam is on a site where nobody will be able to avoid seeing the entire building. CCTV in Beijing is surrounded by tall skyscrapers and therefore dwarfed by other buildings, so that already gives you such different conditions. So it's only OMA's approach in terms of its response to a specific situation.

Name
Rem Koolhaas
Occupation
Architect
Company
OMA
Location
De Rotterdam,
Rotterdam
Date
November 2013

AF You mentioned OMA's current preoccupation is preservation.

RK Basically we work up to levels. We work as architects but we also
constantly try to explore where new issues arise or where new
contradictions emerge or where a particular way of thinking about
a subject is no longer vital and needs revision. Currently we are
thinking about the countryside, because it's a cliché that everyone
is living in the city, so we're preparing for what one could do in the
countryside, perhaps a new way of thinking about the countryside.

In the same way we have been looking at preservation. We've
discovered that a large part of the world is under preservation and
therefore cannot be changed. That made us aware that the world
is divided into areas that change extremely quickly and areas that
cannot change. We're working on the implications of that.

Above
The De Rotterdam
building by OMA

Imogen Heap

'I wanted to do something where I could manipulate my computer wirelessly, so music becomes more like a dance than a robotic act'

Musician Imogen Heap invited us to her home near London to show us her Mi.Mu gesture-control gloves, which allow her to manipulate music live while performing on stage.

Marcus Fairs Tell us about the gloves you've been working on.

Imogen Heap I'm a musician, but more recently I've been developing some gloves with an amazing team of people to help me make music on the move, gesturally, enabling me to interact more naturally with my music software.

MF So they allow you to make music without having to be tied to keyboards or other instruments?

IH Half a performance is spent racing around between instruments and bits of technology on stage. Pressing a record button doesn't look or feel very expressive but actually that moment of recording something is a real creative act. But these actions have always been hidden from the audience and they disengage me in my performance, so I wanted to find a way to do that and integrate it into the performance.

There are so many types of sound that don't have a physical existence. They're software, they're hidden inside the computer. A bassline might sound sculpted; it might have this blobby, stretchy sound. For me it doesn't feel natural to play a sound like that on a keyboard because a keyboard is very restrictive and very linear and you only have two hands. I can play a melody, but if I wanted to manipulate any kind of parameter of that sound, my other hand is completely used up. It's quite restrictive. I wanted to find a way to be really expressive in using this software.

So in order to free myself from my various bits of technology and bridge the gap between the stage and the audience, I wanted something where I could manipulate my computer on the move, wirelessly. So that music becomes more like a dance rather than a robotic act, like pressing a button or moving a fader.

MF How do the gloves work?

IH They have bend sensors in the fingers, lights for feedback, buzzers integrated in the side, so I can sense where I am if I want to get a haptic feedback. They also contain a microprocessor unit that has an accelerometer, a magnetometer and a gyroscope in it.

We've been developing them for about four years and they've come a long way. We started with fibre-optic bend sensors in the fingers but we quickly realised that we needed positional data,

Name
Imogen Heap
Occupation
Musician
Location
Her home,
Essex, UK
Date
March 2014

accelerometer data and gyroscope data, so we could really get inside the music. Because having the bend sensors in the beginning was almost like just pressing buttons. It felt very unnatural. It actually began with little lapel microphones, made by Sennheiser. Seven years ago I began to stick them onto my wrists so that I could make sound with wineglasses or I could play my mbira[1] on stage. I would be able to avoid putting microphones on stage for festivals or touring, so it would cut down on the weight and the transport costs, which is also a reason for the gloves.

In the early versions of the gloves it all connects to a hub that I wear on my upper body. It's all quite complicated but it basically communicates with the computer wirelessly, so I can manipulate music software, unchain myself from the computer, humanise the missing bits of how I interact with technology in music.

I use these gloves with a Kinect[2], so I can have an extra dimension on top of these local gestural movements. I can use the stage as a playground, like different zones for different presets. I could map the centre of the stage for a certain key, and if I go over to the right and combine it with a gesture, I can have a different key or a different set of sounds to play with. I could mute and unmute different instruments that are inside the music software.

There's really nothing out there on the market like this, that enables me to be this expressive with music on the move in the studio and on stage. It's very exciting. When you see me play, when it works, when it's effortless and when your movement is part of the music, it's almost like a dance. Your gestures and how you create that particular sound is so natural that the tech disappears.

MF The newest version of the gloves does away with all the wires and the backpack. How do they work?

IH It's very exciting because it's so much simpler and it needs less gear, less setting up. It's compact and doesn't need so many extra wires. The main reason is this: it has an x-IMU[3], built by Seb Madgwick of X-IO Technologies, containing an accelerometer, a gyroscope and a magnetometer. But the main difference is it now has WiFi built into the glove. So it doesn't need an extra unit to send information to the computer.

That is incredible because it's sending Open Sound Control data instead of serial MIDI data[4]. There are two bend sensors in the wrists and we've still got the bend sensors in the fingers and 'forchettes' between them, telling us how closed or open my hands are and how much my hands are bending. We've found that the bend sensors so far are the simplest solution. But really we want to get to the point where it's all e-textiles, so we can separate the hard tech from the soft tech.

MF What are e-textiles?

IH Electronic textiles. So information is passing through fabric by using conductive threads or materials. This is where we are and

Imogen Heap

1 An mbira is a musical instrument from Africa consisting of a wood board with metal springing keys

2 Kinect is a motion-sensing device for gaming by Microsoft

3 x-IMU is an inertial measurement unit (IMU) that tracks movement, velocity and position

4 Open Sound Control and its predecessor MIDI are technical standards that allow electronic instruments and computers to communicate

it's beautiful and I'm very excited. But at the moment it's really simple – it just sees this exoskeleton as a device and then it comes up on your computer as a WiFi device and you're ready to go.

MF Could the gloves be used for other creative uses besides music?

IH A lot of people have been in touch. One guy suggested he could take all the international sign language, which you only need one hand for, and translate that sonically, so each gesture for a word could be mapped and generate a word. You could actually 'sonify' sign language. You could hack a little speaker onto the system, so it could actually speak for you as well. So that's one idea.

And in the video for Me, the Machine, which is a song I wrote with the gloves and for the gloves, you see me manipulating visuals with them. Just drawing lines onto a screen that's in front of me, so you can see me drawing in real time. It's great fun to do. I can draw little arrows and houses and people. It's not like using a pencil; it's incredible to be able to create these grand shapes, to be able to shift everything, painting out of nothing and spinning it around and stopping it and moving it over here. So I imagine a few people might start to use them with visuals.

That's way in the future, but I think the most important thing is that we feel this urgency from a community that doesn't really exist yet but is there waiting. Which is the main reason why we're looking for funding through crowd-funding website Kickstarter. Originally it was never meant to be a commercial product; it was just going to be for me. But we've developed this amazing thing and it's exciting to see other people have that moment, when they put on the glove and do something simple, like a volume ride or a pan, and feel that direct connection. It's like mainlining music.

MF What about non-creative uses? Could these gloves be used by surgeons, for example, or pilots, or bus drivers?

IH I think there are a lot of applications. You don't have to paint or make music with them. For our Kickstarter campaign, we've been thinking about funny things we could pretend to do with them. So I suppose as long as you can access your computer inside your car, there's no reason why you couldn't just sit in the back of your car and indicate right or left. It's a remote control. It feels like an expressive musical instrument sometimes, but it's essentially a remote control, and anything you could potentially do with your hands, you could do with your gloves.

MF Do you plan to manufacture and sell them as products?

IH We would love for the gloves to be as affordable as something like a MIDI keyboard, in time – something that's as easy to use as MIDI and becomes standard. Because imagine if this was one of those expressive things people would go to when they feel more rigid technology won't do. What's exciting is that they're totally customisable. You can even hack them – you might want a screen,

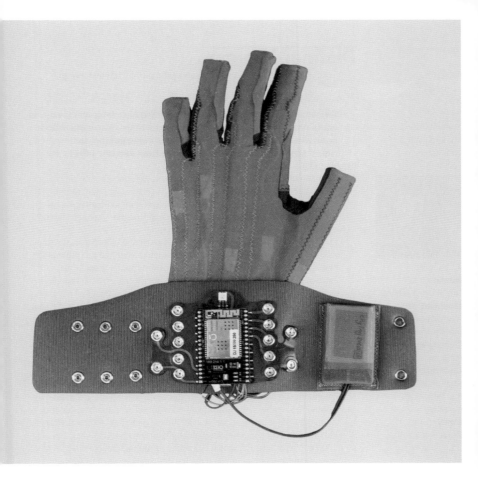

or maybe you'll want a push-button thing, or something that gives off a smell when you move your hand. It's really exciting to see what people might do with hacking them. So the software is going to be open source and so is the hardware. We can't wait to see what people do with them. It's still early stages.

MF There's a lot of talk about wearable technology removing the need for computers. How do your gloves fit into that trend?

IH I don't claim they'll be the answer to every computer interaction, but there are a lot of applications where it just feels wrong to use a keyboard. You might want to build a house. Or you could use some architecture software to draw little windows and move them around like Play-Doh. Maybe we'll get to the point where people will start to develop software like that. That would be amazing.

Above
The Mi.Mu glove, developed by a team led by Imogen Heap

Dietmar Thomas
'This is not a light source. It's more a beautiful material that emits light'

Innovations in OLED technology could see glowing windows and walls replacing traditional lights, says Philips communication specialist Dietmar Thomas. This interview became our most-watched video ever, with more than 180,000 plays.

Name
Dietmar Thomas
Occupation
Communication
specialist
Company
Philips
Location
Philips Lumiblade
Creative Lab,
Aachen
Date
December 2012

Marcus Fairs What is OLED?

Dietmar Thomas OLED is a completely new light source. Until now, every light source on the market has been a point light source, starting with a flame, then the bulb and then the high-powered LED. Now, for the first time, we have a light source where the light comes out of the complete surface.

OLED stands for 'organic light-emitting diode'. Organic does not mean that we're using animals or plants in there. It stands for the organic chemistry in those LEDs – chemicals based on hydrocarbons. It's a chemical light source. So for the first time, people don't need a system to spread the light. With OLEDs, the system is, so to speak, built in.

MF What happens here at the Philips Lumiblade Creative Lab?

DT This light source is so brand new that we had to have outside thinkers work with us to make it the way it is. We opened our labs very early to give designers and architects a first glimpse of our OLEDs. Therefore we installed this Lumiblade Creative Lab. It's a kind of open innovation centre where we invite people from all over to come and experience our light sources and learn more about them. Also, we collaborate with designers, architects and light manufacturers on new ways to bring OLED to the market, to make OLED a household product in a few years.

In the room behind me are some of the products that have been designed here at the Lumiblade Creative Lab by famous designers like Jason Bruges and Tom Dixon. There's Jason Bruges' Mimosa, which imitates flower heads opening and closing. There's our interactive wall, which was co-designed by the digital designers rAndom International in London. These are not just designs, they are also products, because everything we're showing here is already on the market.

MF Let's talk about the light source itself. What's the difference between OLEDs and regular LEDs?

DT Besides the difference that OLEDs are complete light sources, OLEDs have many other features that are different from other light sources. For example they are extremely thin, just 1.8 millimetres at the moment, going even below that soon. More than a light source, this is a beautiful material that emits light. So OLED will not replace existing lighting technologies, but it

will open up completely new ways that a light can be introduced to the customer – integrated into furniture, into other materials and so on. Due to the fact that OLEDs do not get very warm – we're talking about 30 degrees centigrade, maximum – OLEDs can also be used on the surface of drawers or on paper, areas that have been no-gos for other light sources, because those sources get so hot that they would start a fire when used with those materials.

MF What are the possible future uses of OLEDs?

DT There are three things that are going to happen with OLEDs. They are getting larger, they are getting brighter and they are getting more efficient. At the moment the maximum size we can offer our customers is roughly 12 by 12 centimetres, but in the future we will see a square metre panel of OLED, which you can easily integrate into the ceiling or any other material. They are rather new to the market, but we're working on decorative lighting, very beautiful lighting, here at the lab.

Also we have, at this point, only reflective OLEDs. That means that when you switch it off, you see the aluminium backside of it, like a mirror. But the future will also see transparent OLEDs that open up possibilities in the usage. Just imagine windows where transparent OLEDs are integrated. So during the day the sunlight shines into the room and in the evening you're not switching on the ceiling lamp or the wall lamp, but instead you're switching on the window lamp. It's a fantastic thing.

Two years ago, together with the chemical company BASF, we produced a transparent OLED and a transparent solar panel. Combined, they were integrated into a concept car. During the day the driver can see the sky and in the evening, when he needs light, he simply switches on the wonderful glass panels in the roof. So, fantastic things to come.

MF How integrated do you think the OLED will be in our lives?

DT We are now in a niche area with high-end designers, but in three or four years' time, everyone will be able to buy an OLED system at their local lighting store. In the future you will see OLEDs in places where other light sources have never been. It will make our life so different.

MF For example?

DT Cars are one example. If you see the tail-lights of cars today, they use rows of stacked LEDs in order to make a surface light source. Now along comes OLED, which is a surface light source. When a car designer comes to us and says, 'I want to have the OLED in exactly this form and colour,' we can produce that. What will end up in the back of the car is a lovely, natural-looking light in exactly the right tone. The advantage is not only design freedom but construction freedom, too. Because OLEDs are just 1.8 millimetres thick, the extra space can be used for the boot or to make the car shorter.

Dietmar Thomas

In the interior, there are so many ways OLED could play a role for passengers. For example, the vanity mirror. The vanity mirror could be an OLED, so when it's switched off it is reflective but when you switch it on, the light comes out of the mirror itself. So it's a totally new way of bringing light into the car. Also the light can be integrated into the seats, so you don't have to have the ugly plastic caps above light systems, which are used even in luxury cars now. The lights could come out of the sideboards or wherever, so it's a fantastic way to redefine lighting within cars.

The same goes with households. In kitchen systems today, you always see lights under the cupboards. Mostly they are hidden behind ugly wooden systems and you're not meant to see them. The OLED can be integrated into the surface of the kitchen, so the light comes from everywhere, not where you expect it to come from.

In the bathroom, you've got the interactive mirror hanging, then you have the shower. The shower is normally a shield with glass walls, and normally somewhere in the middle of the room there is a light hanging from the ceiling, not giving enough light into the shower itself. Now, integrate transparent OLED into the shower and you not only have a light source there, you have a shield to the outside. No one can look into the shower when the light is switched on.

The same goes for offices. Today, we use fluorescent light systems in the ceiling. Forget about those systems. Simply make them camouflaged. You don't see them at all until you switch them on. Or use transparent OLEDs in larger offices to separate each room. You can have OLEDs at different levels, so you can dim the surrounding area when you have to concentrate. Or you can simply turn it up to full brightness and no one can look into your room.

Replacing systems in the office or living room is what we can expect in the near future. What might be in the far future, five to ten years from now: you are not going to paint your walls with a normal colour; you will use a paint with OLED mixed into it. You paint the wall and when you run an electric current through it, the wall lights up in a nice ambient lighting scheme. Just think about bendable OLEDs, three-dimensional OLEDs, where you can have OLEDs on drinking glasses and the glasses will light up when you add a current to them. The environment of bars might change dramatically.

MF How efficient are they?

DT OLEDs as a young light source have the potential to be very efficient. We are behind LED systems by roughly three years. But you can say that we are going to be roughly 80 percent more efficient than any other light system out there – for example the old-fashioned light bulb.

MF How long do they last?

DT They already have a life span of 15,000 hours. This will get better and better every year. When you see LED systems that have 80,000 hours of life, OLED will be in that area soon.

MF And how much do they cost?

DT The square-metre OLEDs cost between €6000 and €7000. This is rather high. We expect a price drop in the next years to below €1000 per square metre. We're really paving the way to mass-market OLEDs in the next five years, where everyone can buy OLED systems – at IKEA, for example.

Above
Philips'
Lumiblade
LivingShapes
OLED
installation,
co-developed
with rAndom
International

Hussein Chalayan
'I think of London as the New York of Europe. There is this sense of anything being possible'

We interviewed the Turkish Cypriot fashion designer for the Design Museum's Super Contemporary exhibition, which explored London's creative networks. In this extract, he talks about the early days of his career in the city.

Marcus Fairs Can you go back to your early days in London and walk us through your emergence as a designer?

Name
Hussein
Chalayan
Occupation
Fashion designer
Location
Design Museum,
London
Date
June 2009

Hussein Chalayan I first came to London simply because my father lived here and all Turkish Cypriots have a connection with London because we were a colony. I think almost all Turkish Cypriots have come through London at some point in their lives because they have relatives here, they come for holidays, they get educated here, they go back to Cyprus. There has always been a back and forth between Cyprus and London, and with the Greek Cypriots, too.

When I was 18 I started attending the fashion course at Central Saint Martins. In those days it was a big deal to get in, and I was there for four years. I graduated in 1993, not really knowing what I was going to do.

I was asked to do a window at Browns, which at the time was a coveted spot because it had been given to John Galliano ten years earlier, so the press picked up on it. Suddenly I started to get commissions and coverage when I wasn't really planning to do anything. I remember the main buyer at Browns, Joan Burstein, saying to me, 'If you don't do something now with this interest, nothing will happen.' There was a friend whose brother was interested in investing in a new venture and we became partners, so for several years after that, step by step, we grew a business.

We started to show at London Fashion Week, to sell to Japan, and a number of stores bought our stuff, and that would increase every season. Since then, it's just been a journey, to be honest.

MF What was London's fashion industry like in those days?

HC At that time in London, in 1993 or '94, it was just after the recession. There weren't a lot of designers. There wasn't much going on. There was room for new designers: people like Alexander McQueen, myself, Owen Gaster, Copperwheat Blundell, Sonnentag Mulligan. I think there was definitely hunger for new designers to come up. I think, in a way, now there are too many designers. At that time it was easier to shine and we were doing interesting work as well.

It was an exciting time. There was the beginning of the Young British Artists[1] thing as well – there were parallel things going on. I remember at the time being very strongly supported by Björk. She was wearing my stuff to concerts and was really a sort of force. There was a stronger interconnection with music and with video, this atmosphere existed where people helped one another out a bit more. Even though it was behind the scenes, it had an effect.

Through magazines like Wallpaper, different facets of life got closer and closer aesthetically, like interiors would be shown in the same magazine as fashion, which was also showing industrial design. Then the late '90s emerged and in a way everything became more mass. Although there's now this connection – visually, aesthetically, maybe superficially – between the different worlds, at the time it was genuinely about everyone starting at the same time together. We had more of a connection, which had an effect.

MF What was it about London that created such an interesting crop of designers?

HC London has always been a place where the best music, a lot of good artists, a lot of good films, so many good things have come out. I think the fact that London is a multicultural place, that adds to the mix and the openness of it all. There is definitely a kind of Anglo-Saxon acceptance of everything that sets London apart from other cities in Europe.

I think of London as the New York of Europe. Because of the history of colonialism, England has had to bear the influx of immigration for a longer period of time than most other countries, so there is this sense of anything being possible here. Something like having Nasser Hussain[2] as the cricket captain – it is only just happening now in other parts of the world. There is this situation where anyone can come from anywhere and still achieve things.

Part of my work is inspired by London, in the sense that London, for me, is like the background I come from. I'm from an island and we have a very mixed history. We identify with Turkey even though we have our own government in northern Cyprus. Just like in some ways we've identified with Sicily, even though Sicily is part of Italy. We come from a mixed background where we don't know any more who our ancestors are, because the idea of the nation-state is always there to wipe out the differences.

Coming here, because the history of immigration is more recent, you can still detect the differences. You have Chinatown, you have the Jewish areas, you have the Korean area, the Turkish area and you can enjoy those different textures. But where I come from, over a longer period of time, it has melted and you can't separate it.

I enjoy the variety of people here, partly because it's innate in me, so I have a strong interest in movements of people across time, across land. London life keeps that innate curiosity alive for me because I can really enjoy all the differences.

1 Young British Artists (YBAs) is the name given to a group of visual artists including Damien Hirst and Tracey Emin

2 Indian-born Nasser Hussain was the captain of England's cricket team from 1999 until 2003

Formafantasma
'We are never really interested in the technical side but in the ability of objects to evoke memories'

Andrea Trimarchi and Simone Farresin of Formafantasma represent a new direction in Italian design, despite being based in the Netherlands. As part of the Peroni Collaborazioni series of talks, we spoke to them about their relationship with Italy and their work with cereal and natural plastics.

Marcus Fairs Tell us about your work, influences and background.

Andrea Trimarchi We are an Italian studio based in Eindhoven. Me and Simone met in Florence while studying at ISIA[1], which was the first design school in Italy, born after the economic boom of the 1960s. After that we decided to leave Italy and to go the Design Academy in Eindhoven to do the Innovation Management Masters. We graduated from there in 2009.

Simone Farresin Florence is a beautiful place to study. The school was also interesting because our teachers, Paolo Deganello and Gilberto Corretti, were founders of the radical Archizoom movement[2]. It was interesting that they were so involved in it, because in our work there are some critical and political elements that we can connect with those origins. On the other hand, Florence is a beautiful place. It's easy to get lazy, physically.

MF Why did you decide to base yourselves in Eindhoven?

SF When we graduated from ISIA, we thought we needed to move abroad. We needed to experience our collaboration in a different environment. We felt this necessity to engage with a different kind of design that wasn't happening in Italy. Eindhoven is a really small town in the southeast of Holland. Quite ugly, uninteresting, in a way. It's kind of an environment where we had, for the first time, no visual noises, no heritage.

AT And it actually helped us a lot to look back to our origins, in a way.

SF In Italy you have this great generation of masters. Then when you are studying there, you have all these people teaching you the right way of doing design, because you have these great examples. In Holland, it's completely different, because the most recent design scene is not so much linked to the past as the Italian one.

Eindhoven gave us the possibility to have our own studio, in a former mental hospital, that we managed to turn into a more welcoming environment to work and live in. We can always say that in our work, as we mentioned, there are some critical and political elements that are an evolution of what happened in the 1970s in Italy, but also it's the fruit of the conceptual design scene that has been growing in the Netherlands since the 1990s.

Names
Andrea Trimarchi and Simone Farresin

Occupation
Industrial designers

Company
Formafantasma

Location
RIBA, London

Date
April 2012

MF One of your best-known projects is Autarchy, which consisted of a series of vessels made from flour.

AT Autarchy is a project from 2010 that was presented by Spazio Rossana Orlandi during the Salone del Mobile in Milan. Everything started when we visited this small town in Sicily called Salemi, which once a year produces an enormous quantity of bread. They do this quite kitsch bread with quite naïve but really intricate decoration. And they attach it to big architectural structures.

SF So what we thought was interesting there, and it happens a lot in our work, is that our references are not coming from industrial Italy but more from rural cultures. We were not really interested in the results of what they were doing but more the idea of this community, that they just use what they know. And they meet once a year to produce, to engage. We imagine they are re-engaging with production, in a way.

So we wanted to translate these ideas in a different way, and we did this Autarchy installation, where we are questioning the way we are engaged with production. Autarchy is both a material research but it's also the portrait of a utopian scenario. The vases were composed with 70 percent flour, 20 percent agriculture waste and ten percent limestone.

AT And all the colour is obtained by filtering and boiling different kinds of spices and vegetables.

SF So we wanted biodegradable materials that were natural, but most of all that were easily found and used. A characteristic of our work is that we are never really interested in the technical side of it, but more in the ability that objects and materials have to either evoke memories or to incorporate narrative elements.

MF You've experimented with other biodegradable materials. Your Botanica project investigated a range of natural plastics.

AT Botanica is a sort of second chapter of Autarchy. After we finished Milan, we got in contact with this really nice lady from a foundation called Plart in Italy. Plart is interesting because it's the first foundation in Europe that is meant for the restoration and recovery of plastic objects. When we received this phone call from her we were quite surprised, because we had done Autarchy, which was a project that was almost the opposite of plastic. Because, of course, we were also victims of our own prejudice about plastic. We had in mind, you know, plastic bottles or the enormous patch of plastic debris that's in the middle of the ocean.

SF And then we researched a specific moment in time that we call the pre-Bakelite period, before oil was involved in the production of plastics. In that period, between the eighteenth and nineteenth centuries, a lot of researchers and scientists were looking to the natural world in search of plasticity. So we found amazing materials like *bois durci*, which is a mixture of animal blood and sawdust. DNA is a polymer, so with high pressures and vapour

Formafantasma

1 The ISIA is the
Higher Institute for
Artistic Industries
in Florence, Italy

2 Archizoom
Associati was an
influential design
studio founded
in Florence in 1966
by architects and
designers including
Andrea Branzi and
Massimo Morozzi

DNA binds the fibres of wood together. And then natural shellac, used in restoration, is taken from the excrement of insects that colonise trees, and that's mixed with wood fibres.

What we thought was interesting was to use this project to raise questions about the way we deal with evolution and how old production methods can have a relevance in contemporary time. The research was really long – we started in August and ended in March – so we had only one month to produce the pieces.

At the end we managed to turn it into a coherent body of work, where our main interest was imagining almost a fictional moment in time and wondering what would have happened to these materials if oil-based plastic was not invented.

MF How did the properties of these natural polymers influence the forms you designed?

AT The first object we designed was an archetypal vase shape. But working with the material, we were starting to look at how it was speaking to us. So we decided to leave all this kind of tongue or leaf that was coming from the material itself. That was interesting, because they are the result of the process of the making.

MF The last project I want to talk about is actually one of your first.

AT Moulding Tradition is our graduation project. We went to this city in the middle of Sicily called Caltagirone. It's a special place because more than 300 artisans are still working in ceramics there – a lot if you consider that it's a really small city.

MF Sicily seems to be a constant in your work.

SF We have an interest, almost an obsession, with Sicily. Andrea is Sicilian, but it's interesting because it's an island and there is not such an industrial component there. Craft is still really relevant.

And while we were there we got almost obsessed with a specific artefact, this strange vase with a face of an African. In Sicily it's really common to see these pieces. You walk on the street and see on balconies vases with a face of an African. You wonder, 'Why is this piece somehow symbolising Sicilian culture?'

Then researching it we find out it is referring to the tenth century, when African Arabs conquered Sicily and imported maiolica ceramics. So this is somehow an homage to this specific invasion, to the origins of these materials. But then, this piece is reminding us of what is happening now in contemporary time.

We thought it was grotesque, because almost daily, 500 illegal immigrants are trying to enter the EU from north Africa. So we find ourselves really debating a lot and wondering, 'Shall we just ignore this part of the story? Or shall we embrace it, incorporating these different notions and different ideas?'

We decided on the second option. We designed pieces that are pretty archetypal. We went to the museum in Caltagirone and we sampled original pieces and layered different meanings into the ceramic. But we substituted the element of grotesque in the

original piece with a portrait of an existing refugee. And we added textual information that is either describing the first immigration flows, the first conquerors of Sicily, or the new immigration flows.

For us, this is a way to debate how we deal with tradition. In Italy, tradition is everything. But we have a complex relationship with this idea, because as much as we work with craft, as much as we think it's important to relate with tradition, we also see the downside.

Moulding Tradition is a way to question the relationship we have with tradition because the original piece is reminding us how much immigration flows are important in the formation of Italian culture. And on the other side we use craft as a way to justify and to protect traditions.

Suzanne Lee
'Would you wear leather as a vegan if the animal didn't die for it?'

In the future, clothing will be grown in laboratories rather than manufactured from plant or animal products, according to the founder of fashion research laboratory BioCouture.

Dan Howarth Why are you researching ways of growing materials?

Suzanne Lee My training is actually in fashion but I'm really interested in how new technologies can challenge designers about how we create. Through an engagement with biology, I'm really excited about how we can think of organisms like microbes as the factories of the future, and how you can take something like a yeast cell and design that to produce a material. As a designer, collaborating with scientists and engineers, you can design better, smarter materials and envision new kinds of sustainable products.

DH How do you grow a garment?

SL The recipe I've been exploring is using a symbiotic mix of yeast and bacteria. It's a fermentation method that grows bacterial cellulose. But the particular recipe gives you something very flexible, kind of like vegetable leather, if you like.

BioCouture as a consultancy is interested in this emerging landscape of living materials. Looking at organisms like bacteria, yeast, fungi, algae... there's a whole spectrum of organisms that can grow material for us. We're starting to see that impact across many different material sectors. I'm interested in apparel, sport, luxury and beauty, but there are also people looking at packaging, construction, furniture, architecture. And we're at the dawn of a new industry in petrochemical alternatives, something that is sustainable and biodegradable with enhanced performance.

DH What have you already produced using this method?

SL BioCouture is pioneering bacterial cellulose: creating fibres in a vat of liquid instead of taking fibres from a plant source. Most people know BioCouture for a series of garments that were grown using bacteria, so the fibres, materials and formation of the garment were done by a microbe rather than a plant. That's a radical shift away from how we've previously imagined a piece of clothing.

The challenge in that is, how would you scale it up industrially? There are issues around cost and the fact that there are no existing bio-facilities that would enable you to produce in an economically viable way. So I think that's where some of the other industry sectors are going to be the first to market with a grown material.

DH What's different about these garments in terms of how they feel and how you wear them?

SL Bacterial cellulose is still a very experimental material. But what attracts me to it is that it's completely compostable. It's not just

Name
Suzanne Lee
Occupation
Fashion designer
Company
BioCouture
Location
Wearable
Futures
conference,
London
Date
December 2013

biodegradable. You could throw it away like your vegetable peelings. And obviously we have major issues around toxicity and pollution throughout the supply chain of textile production. What that's proposing is a radical way of producing something sustainable. It's a biological material, so in terms of fast fashion, there's less reason for guilt. You can actually grow it from a waste stream. If you can train microbes to feed on waste, you're potentially upcycling. So you take waste and grow something useful, but at the end of its life you can just discard it and it will nourish the soil.

In terms of functionality, I think where it gets interesting is where you begin to imbue that organism with new qualities. We're interested in the area of synthetic biology and how we might design optimised organisms that will not only grow as a fibre but grow in the colour we need, so we don't need to dye it. How can you bring the DNA from other organisms with desirable traits into somewhere so you can have this optimised microbial factory?

DH So what are you working on next? What's the next step?

SL There are multiple directions. One is working with clients who are also innovating living materials. We function as a catalyst between the materials innovations and the brands and designers who are looking for new, sustainable materials. Some of that is quite close to market. Then there are other projects I would say are near-term, maybe five years away. And there are long-term projects where we collaborate with academic labs, pushing the boundaries of synthetic biology. We're imagining designing organisms that will produce the living materials of the future. Then across that we're forecasting trends: where and how these materials might be used.

DH You're currently doing a project with Selfridges in London.

SL For our Selfridges project we're growing a skirt. Hopefully it will look like a very convincing garment you might find on a rail at Selfridges, except that it's been grown using bacterial fermentation. At the same time we're going to have a large fermentation tank that will show the material growing, so hopefully there will be a juxtaposition where shoppers will see this strange lab environment with this very unappealing material being grown and then, hopefully, something quite beautiful as an end result: a garment that's been created, that we've never seen before.

DH How likely are we to be wearing lab-grown clothes in the future?

SL Thinking about how this becomes something for the future is a real challenge. There's no coincidence that new developments in fibres and fashion take a really long time to happen. Usually they take millions of dollars of research, and even then it's radically challenging to the consumer and needs to overcome cultural issues.

We're moving towards a landscape where materials can be grown in the laboratory – like the idea that we might grow leather in the lab. Real leather. We're taking live cells from an animal via a biopsy, then growing materials without the death of an animal. So we're going to encounter new ethical questions for things like clothing. Would a vegan wear leather if the animal didn't die for it? Things like that are going to be interesting to communicate.

In the short term it's easier to think about these materials for harder accessories, like footwear, rather than the soft, knitted, woven ones because, unfortunately, those tend to have lower value. Economics is really going to be the first barrier to these kinds of materials because your research and development costs are so high, but the retail cost is so low, you can't recoup the research and development. If you have a material that can sell at a high price, like leather, it begins to make sense.

DH In your talk earlier you mentioned 3D-printing some of these materials. How would that work?

SL The proliferation of 3D printing enables us to think about designing things for ourselves, but the availability of materials is still limited. We've begun to look into processes like bio-printing, which are being spun out of biomedical fields. You might print cells with a nutrient solution that over time will grow together, maybe in layers, with multiple layers of functionality.

The first stage of 3D printing has clearly been about using synthetics, but the future generations of materials we print with will be more organic, and I think that's where it becomes much more exciting – certainly from a sustainability point of view but also from a functionality point of view.

DH How far away from that do you think we are?

SL That's such a difficult question. I don't really want to put a date on it. There are funding and ethical considerations. But once the technology is put out there, it's surprising how quickly that can move. The founders of Google and Facebook are interested in things like growing meat, so who knows? With enough money thrown at a problem, innovation really speeds up.

DH Do you have a vision of the future, maybe in 50 or 100 years' time? How will we be using, producing and making clothes?

SL People always sound ridiculous when they put dates on things because they always get it wrong. But one of the things I'm interested in right now is exploring the quantified self and examining our own biological data. If we think about capturing our own microbiome, the healthy bacteria that is living on us, how much can we begin to incorporate that into clothing? If clothing is sitting on the surface of the human body and it's interacting with that microbiome, how can we think about harnessing the good qualities of the microbiome into those surfaces that surround the body?

That's a whole area that is open for exploration. But you can imagine in the future something like a piece of clothing or

accessory actually having an active interaction with your body. Right now what we have is living organisms making us materials; after the organism is killed, the material exists just like any other. But I can imagine we will eventually move toward the material actually living while it's on you and having a direct relationship to your body in its happy microbiome environment. And perhaps it's diagnosing, treating or nourishing, in some way, the body surface, becoming part of your wellbeing.

Above
BioCouture's BioSkirt, created using microbes rather than plant fibres

Patrick Seguin
'I think Prouvé is essential. Before Prouvé, Modernism was tubes'

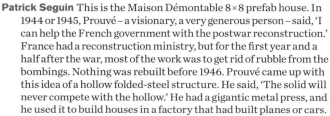

Pioneering Modernist Jean Prouvé developed a series of prefabricated houses in the 1940s to help France's postwar reconstruction effort. Gallerist Patrick Seguin explains why the designs were ahead of their time.

Marcus Fairs Tell us the story of the Prouvé house you're exhibiting at Design Miami.

Name
Patrick Seguin
Occupation
Art dealer
Company
Galerie Patrick Seguin
Location
Design Miami, Miami
Date
December 2013

1 The compass is the two-legged structural centrepiece of the house, supporting the roof truss

Patrick Seguin This is the Maison Démontable 8 × 8 prefab house. In 1944 or 1945, Prouvé – a visionary, a very generous person – said, 'I can help the French government with the postwar reconstruction.' France had a reconstruction ministry, but for the first year and a half after the war, most of the work was to get rid of rubble from the bombings. Nothing was rebuilt before 1946. Prouvé came up with this idea of a hollow folded-steel structure. He said, 'The solid will never compete with the hollow.' He had a gigantic metal press, and he used it to build houses in a factory that had built planes or cars.

But there was a lot of reticence toward industry after the war. Prouvé was pro-industry. He said, 'Three people can build this house in one day.' He had a factory in Nancy, which was hardly damaged by the bombings. So he said, 'I'll prefab houses in my factory.' They could send three trucks a day, each with three people, and three families could get a house in a day. It was genius. There was a programme of 160 houses, but few were built and most were destroyed or reused. There was a lack of metal and wood, so people used the wall panels as tables, the steel to repair tractors.

MF How many of these are surviving?

PS There are two houses like this. One was Prouvé's atelier. It's been protected by the French government, classified as a historical monument. This is the second one, the only other one that exists.

The house comes in ten crates. You open the crate, build the floor. The compass[1] is freestanding. Each piece can be moved by hand by two people. We built this in two days. The six-by-six-metre version can be built in a day. You fix the compass, bolt the crossbeam. Everything is less than ten kilos, very light, very simple.

MF How important was Prouvé?

PS I think Prouvé is essential. Before Prouvé, Modernism was tubes. He had this huge press, four metres long. Two people could hold a sheet of metal and this machine would fold it, bend it, corrugate it.

He was thinking about ecology even before the term existed. He wrote that architecture should leave no trace on the landscape. He was born in Nancy, which was the city of Art Nouveau. But Prouvé hated Art Nouveau. Prouvé had this philosophy of form follows function. There were no decorative elements.

MF There's been a resurgence of interest in Prouvé. His furniture has been reissued by Vitra.

PS Vitra is one of the greatest brands for reproducing, but my interest is in vintage. This is very emotional, very authentic. I recall 25 years ago when it was hard to sell a Prouvé chair for 800 francs. But today, 95 percent of my clients are contemporary art collectors. Because Prouvé is minimalistic, it creates the perfect dialogue.

MF And this house is $2.5 million, is that right?

PS Yes. But you can have one of the six-by-six-metre versions, which are extremely important, for $800,000.

MF There's no kitchen or bathroom, so how do you live in it?

PS You adapt it. You can substitute the wood panels with glass. You can adapt it with an architect. Ask Jean Nouvel – he'll do it for you.

Above
Jean Prouvé's
Maison
Démontable 8×8
prefab house

Job Smeets

'When you try to separate art from design, in effect you're creating a ghetto. Let's not have borders in the creative world'

We spoke to the Dutch artist about how Studio Job rode the design-art boom and how the recession affected the design world.

Marcus Fairs Your work is very distinctive – very different from the things you normally see at design shows.

Job Smeets Some say our work is different. I don't know, I just do the work. I just do my stinking best and try to be genuine and innovative and authentic. Not even innovative – that sounds so technical. It was very simple: when we started out we wanted creative freedom. The only way to reach creative freedom was to start design-sculpture. It's perfect for creation because every time you create you can design a new piece, and even produce it yourself. Otherwise you're dependent on others – you're dependent on the guys who have that machine, you're dependent on another guy who invests in lasers. I just wanted to do anything, to be free.

We started to create clay pieces and cast them in bronze, because in bronze you can make any shape you like. Of course plastic is for the industry and bronze is for the art world, so there was a little issue there. But I thought, 'Okay, let's turn that little issue into something beautiful and introduce sculptural design,' and that's what we did. I'm a happy artist. I'm a happy designer. What more could you want?

MF What's the difference between art and design?

JS I don't have any distinction in my mind between being an artist and being a designer. I really don't care what I am. When you are trying to separate the art from the design, in effect you are creating a ghetto and that's always a bad thing to create, to create borders. We know that from politics. At least let's not have borders in the art world and the creative world.

MF Your work became extremely popular during the design-art boom a few years ago. Tell us about that period and how the market has changed now, in a time of recession.

JS Our market did not change a lot. We have a small company but we have a global company, so when there's a crisis in England and the United States, it doesn't mean there's a crisis in Russia or in other countries. Of course the market changed, because the US wasn't the biggest market any more. But we are a very small ship, so we are of leaner means. A totally new market appeared, at

Name
Job Smeets
Occupation
Artist
Company
Studio Job
Location
Moooi's
Unexpected
Welcome
exhibition, Milan
Date
April 2013

144

least in the Asian counties and in Russia. I don't think our work changed. Maybe the client changed but, in the end, what can a client do? He can buy it but he can never really have it. It will always stay mine.

MF What do you mean by 'it will always stay mine'?

JS People can buy or show my pieces, but they will always stay my pieces whether I have them physically or not. So in the end, it doesn't matter to which part of the world they go, as long as they are good.

MF Has the shifting market encouraged you to diversify into less sculptural work?

JS Yes, but I must say that it's the same thing in fashion. Like haute couture and prêt-à-porter. You can compare a furniture brand

Above
The Bucket
Floor Lamp
by Studio Job
for Moooi

Job Smeets

like Moooi to a fashion brand like Maison Martin Margiela – bigger than a unique piece, but still a small body of work.

With our sculptural pieces, those occupy more or less the haute couture side of our business. The prêt-à-porter pieces are the pieces that we display here at shows like this one, but they all need one another. I think that when you walk into a space that only has our sculptures, you need to fill up the spaces in between them with words – to make sentences, let's say. When you only have beautiful words, connected to one another, you don't have a sentence. You need those little words in between to make the vocabulary.

MF Tell us about some of the 'little words' you've produced for Moooi, that have been chosen for this exhibition.

JS We have worked with Moooi since 2006, I believe, and we started off doing the Paper Furniture collection for them. That was a little distraction from the work I had been doing earlier. We made

'When I was at design school I didn't have the money for expensive materials, so I went to the shop, got boxes and made furniture out of them'

all these unique pieces from paper because I thought that paper made a nice contrast with the bronze, which is otherwise so heavy and paper is really light in comparison. But also, when I was at the Design Academy in Eindhoven I didn't have the money to be able to afford expensive materials, so I went to the shop and asked for some boxes and made some furniture out of them.

And on the other hand, the first thing you learn in kindergarten is to fold little bits of paper, to work with paper. So this is a very authentic approach.

The paper furniture was a very nice success and, on a cultural level, very interesting. They come flatpacked but they are still monumental pieces.

Then I decided it was time to do a chair because we don't have chairs at Studio Job, only bronze chairs, which cost a fortune. So we did a medieval chair in plastic and Moooi produced it in ten different colours. It looked really industrial. It turned out really interesting.

Then I thought, 'Let's do some German hand-painted furniture,' and then we did some of that, too. They're all Moooi hand-painted pieces. In a way the pieces were becoming a bit more sculptural. Even the Bucket Lamp series, for instance, is a mixture of brass, industrial brass, of wood, of paper – it's a really interesting mix.

I think that the pieces we do for Moooi and the pieces that we produce are becoming a bit more sculptural because we're allowed to do shit like that. Five years ago, if I had come to somebody with a bucket balanced upside-down on a wooden pedestal, we wouldn't be here right now. So now we can do it. I think it's to do with trust. We're getting old. People tend to trust you when you're over 40.

Name
Sadie Morgan
Occupation
Architect
Company
de Rijke
Marsh Morgan
Architects
(dRMM)
Location
Inside
Festival,
Singapore
Date
October 2013

Sadie Morgan
'Women want spaces that reflect our needs. And architects have to start responding to that'

One of Britain's leading architects discusses how women with spending power are demanding different architectural spaces – and the controversy surrounding foreign investment in the British housing market.

Marcus Fairs What's your view on the role of women working in architecture today?

Sadie Morgan I think women are the next big thing. We've always been part of most successful businesses, but it's only recently we are coming to the fore – particularly in the architecture profession. If you look at our business, 80 percent of my particular practice is female, and obviously I'm one of the principals. But at the moment women like me are few and far between. Many women have reached the top level of the profession. However, I think many more are waiting in the wings and I think if we can open up opportunities and allow women to come through, it will happen.

MF Why are there so few women in architecture? What can change and what is changing?

SM The perception may be that there are few women in architecture, but I think there are, in fact, a lot. They're generally not at the higher echelons, they're not running businesses. What they're doing is making everything happen. A lot of our project architects in the office are women, but it's taking time to filter through. In my generation, for example, there are increasingly more women – Deborah Saunt, Alison Brooks – running successful practices, and very few other than the Zaha Hadids and Amanda Levetes of the world in the generation above. But among the younger generations, there are a lot more practices run by women.

MF What has kept women out of high-level positions within the profession for so long?

SM Traditionally it's not necessarily a profession that women would have gone into. The construction industry hasn't been that female friendly. It's changed its ways on the surface, but there are still a lot of preconceptions, lots of old-school stuff. There are lots of jobs for the boys, in the generation that isn't used to having women around. But eventually they will have to change. When they realise the best graduates are women, things will change.

MF Another speaker at the Inside Festival said that women are the next big emerging market. Do you agree?

SM In terms of women having spending power? Look: five years ago it was the pink pound, wasn't it? We were looking at the gay market as people who had time and money. I think women are now much more self-possessed. They have the ability, they're professionals, they have the money and, my goodness, do we have the energy. We are absolutely fired up. We want spaces that reflect our needs and our preoccupations. And architects and developers, those people building the hotels, the retail, the housing, I think they have to start responding to a much more feminine and female-orientated community.

SM I think if you were focusing your design purely on women, then yes, it would be very different. There are certain things that we are more or less interested in, in terms of how we live. We have greater preoccupations about our health and wellbeing. We like environments that aren't too flashy, that aren't saying, 'Hello.'

We like environments that are more interactive – girls like to get on and meet and greet and talk while boys are more restrained and enjoy environments that, I think, respond to that. Girls need environments that aren't too stuffy and that are much more

'There are
a lot of women
in architecture
but they're generally
not at the higher
echelons. What
they are doing
is making
everything happen'

relaxed. We want to be treated well. If we are going to a hotel that we're paying to stay in, we want to make sure that responds to what we want – not necessarily what our husbands want, the ones who are traditionally paying for it. They're not. We are. We're paying for ourselves.

SM Exactly. When I go to a hotel, I don't generally go with my family. I go with my girlfriends. We, as a group of girls, have some money.

Sadie Morgan   We want to treat ourselves. We don't necessarily want to bring along our husbands or family to get in the way. We girls want to go and have fun. So in that sense, if there is a hotel with a floor given over to women only, my god, we'd be there. We don't want to be hassled by men, we just want to have a good time. I think it's so special to have spaces that are women-centric, that I could see it would be a massive hit.

MF Your office is working on a lot of housing projects in London. Tell us about those.

SM At the moment, the London housing market is absolutely buoyant. There is lots of work coming through, not only in the pipeline but being built at the moment. We're responsible for three of the early phases in the Elephant & Castle development, the King's Cross development and the Battersea Power Station development. We're finding that all the housing and work we're doing is being pre-sold outside the UK, but that investment and money coming into the UK is allowing house builders to feel confident and invest and start building, which for us can only be good news.

MF Are we talking about the UK or specifically about London?

SM It's only London. The London housing market is actually the only one that's buoyant. It's a little bubble, if you like, in that very few projects are taking off outside the London area. So the investment is absolutely just going into the capital city. If you look at other big cities like Birmingham and Manchester, they are really struggling to get that same level of interest and capital investment that London has.

MF Where is that money coming from, and why is it coming into London?

SM In terms of Battersea, the money that's coming in is from Malaysia – a Malaysian conglomerate is funding that scheme. For other projects, the funding is coming from UK developers but they're confident that they are going to sell it and they're tending to sell it within the Asian market.

I think that money is coming to London because of the crisis with the Euro. Very few countries want to invest within the European currency. The UK has always been seen as an island economy and one that, at the moment, isn't reflective of any of the troubles that are going on, so it's still seen as a safe pair of hands for people's investment.

MF I've heard that some of these housing developments are being advertised in China, Malaysia and Singapore and not in the UK at all. How are these projects being marketed?

SM The last of our two major projects is exclusively being marketed outside the UK – not to say that it's not open to UK buyers, but the first port of call for the developers has been the Asian markets. Nearly all of those apartments for sale are being purchased outside the UK.

That said, 30 percent of the projects we do have go to affordable or shared ownership, as it is called in the UK. I know it's controversial, but the most important thing to say is that it means houses are being built for Londoners in a way that is being funded outside the UK economy.

The government, for its own reasons, isn't doing what it should be doing, which is building low-cost, affordable housing for everybody. Local authorities are getting better at it and the government is giving money to local authorities to do it themselves, but it's been a slow process. It's not happening quickly enough. But the money that's coming in from outside the UK is actually enabling local authorities to charge developers, to say, 'You need to give us the affordable element in this scheme.'

Above
Visualisation of a housing project at the Battersea Power Station in London, by dRMM

Sadie Morgan

MF Traditionally, affordable housing and luxury housing would be in the same development. So, as an architect, are you being asked to separate them?

SM The Asian market likes to have separate privately-owned and affordable housing. Our practice has always worked hard to integrate. We don't like the kind of ghettoism of splitting up communities: you're rich, you have this area of London and you can't afford it, so you live somewhere else. I think the most wonderful thing about London is not only the cultural mix but the mix of all different types in the community.

And, ironically, that's what people buy into – that crazy London scene, which has everybody mixed up in one big pot together, living next to one another. I think that's what gives

'The last of our two major housing projects is exclusively being marketed outside the UK. The first port of call for the developers is the Asian market'

London its richness and that's what gives the perception, for those looking in, of a society that enjoys community and is receptive.

The developers who are insisting social housing be taken out are creating a rod for their own back, because they will create communities that don't really exist, and people don't want to buy into an empty apartment block and be the only person living there. They want to have a sense of people around them, a real fixed community, not a transient one. I think it's important as architects to still try and force, as best we can, developers to make sure the mix is there.

MF You mentioned having to design to Asian standards. How does this affect the way you design buildings?

SM We're finding that having a space for community is something the Asian culture brings to the UK. In lots of apartments, we're asked to build spaces like ancillary rooms that can be used by groups of people, which is fantastic. There are other needs such as a concierge, and the sense of luxury is always there, whether that be through materiality or through the linkages of the types of spaces.

Asian standards are not really about size or space. What we do, sometimes, is make sure there are always bathrooms – more bathrooms than you would generally have. In the UK, we would normally have one or two, but we're now seeing a big push toward having more bathrooms.

MF A lot of people are critical of others coming in and buying up housing that they think should go to local people, and driving up prices in the process. How do you feel about that?

SM I feel very passionately that the UK should build its own housing. I think governments should be responsible for building good housing for people who don't necessarily want to buy, or first-time buyers. They need to build affordable housing for everybody. I think developers are doing what they have always done, which is look to people to invest in their business. If the government isn't investing, they can find outside investors. That means we'll get housing built and a percentage of it is given back to us as a community, which I think is a good thing.

I think it's not the fault of people who want to bring money into the UK. It's the fault of the government, frankly, for not building sustainable housing for the UK economy. If you reflect on buildings that are seen to be completely empty, I think that is problematic. You don't want transient communities. You want long-term, sustainable communities.

Naoto Fukasawa
'Italian people share the Japanese mentality. It's a good combination'

The Japanese industrial designer told us how new technology is changing the way people use furniture in this interview conducted in Milan during the Salone del Mobile.

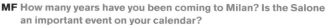

Marcus Fairs What will you be presenting this week in Milan?

Naoto Fukasawa This year I have been working with many of the Italian companies, designing things for Magis and Vitra. There is also an interesting collection for a Japanese company called Maruni, a very nice wood company, which we're showing in Milan, too. Other new things are for Viccarbe, a Spanish company. I work for 15 different companies.

MF How many years have you been coming to Milan? Is the Salone an important event on your calendar?

NF The Salone is kind of the core festival of the European design community. There are not only Milan-based companies participating. It's more worldwide. I happened to come first ten years ago.

I'm trying to design more iconic projects, with particular focus on the brand. I don't really design in different ways for each different company; I'm always using the same minimalist design. However I try to understand the company and the image. It's kind of like the spicy things you put on the food you like. That's why I'm still working with the same companies, even after ten years.

MF Do you think your minimalist approach comes from your being Japanese?

NF It's a more integrated harmony. Life is not so divided. In Japan our mind is very different but our body is experiencing the same lifestyle. Japan is a very good country, it has very good technologies and also very good service and product quality. So that has naturally influenced me. I bring those qualities to Italy. But Italian people also share the Japanese mentality. It's a good combination.

MF Some people don't understand why minimalist, designer furniture is more expensive than ordinary furniutre.

NF The body is more happy when we are choosing the right things. When you go into a café, for example, you are spontaneously choosing the right table for a cup of coffee, so that's part of the design. Those are the tiny things that make our lives happy without paying any money. People have to pay more attention to see the quality of life, not measuring it by money. With quality furniture, people don't need to spend so much money to have a good-quality space. These are long-lasting products. They can be with people all their lives.

Name
Naoto Fukasawa
Occupation
Industrial
designer
Location
B&B Italia
showroom, Milan
Date
April 2013

MF Which of these projects has been the most successful?

NF I don't really know which is the best product in the beginning, because it is not out in life yet. Only after a few years, if people keep it and like it, I will know.

MF What would you say was the best product you ever designed?

NF I have done lots of popular designs for Muji. Everyone knows the CD player that is attached on the wall – that is what everyone recognises my name for. Some people recognise my name through the Papilio furniture for B&B Italia, and the Hiroshima furniture for Maruni. I've also done an Android mobile phone. An interface designer, Yugo Nakamura[1], participated on this design with me, but it's hardware and software integrated, a really clever thing.

Above
The Papilio
bed by Naoto
Fukasawa for
B&B Italia. The
butterfly-shaped
headboard
allows you to
watch TV in bed

Naoto Fukasawa

1 Yugo Nakamura
is a Japanese web
designer who
pioneered the
use of complex
interactive
animations in
websites

MF What brand is the phone?

NF It's a brand called AU, a Japanese company. Initially I made a mobile phone for AU called Infobar – Information Bar. That was very small, but the technology has improved now that they're using an Android-based model, the Infobar A02. I worked with Yugo Nakamura to develop an Android interface, which is very unique. I also designed the sound. I worked with very good digital-technology musicians to compose the noises emitted by the phone as users swipe around the interface. We can say this is a tablet PC. Technology has become more organic. Everything is integrated within a very tiny box.

MF What's unique about the phone?

NF It's Android-based – so that is not so different, because now many smartphones have the same Android operating system. But the movement of the interactive tiles on the screen, the way you can manipulate them, is very intuitive. People don't need to read a manual. It's not difficult logic. It's designed for single-handed operation and it's fun to use. It's partly graphic design, partly interaction design. Everybody says 'Wow' when they use it.

MF What is the future of these kinds of technologies?

NF I don't really know. Someone is seriously developing these kinds of things, but also they doubt whether it has a future life or not. A driver needs better navigation or a more safe driving system, but those technologies will be more invisible. The function is there, but it's not a physical box any more. Digital technology used

'This chair is for computing; this bed is for watching TV. That's my way of connecting technology and furniture'

to have a core mechanism in a box. The size of the object was huge. Technology engineers are naturally trying to eliminate some of this form while the content is growing up.

MF So technology is becoming more integrated?

NF The environment and the lifestyle, those things now have to be integrated with technology. We need to think more about transportation in cities and architects designing walls that will be more intelligent, to communicate, that don't need particular heating systems or cooling systems or speakers – where everything is already there inside. Intelligence should be built into the product.

MF Do you think technology will become part of furniture?

NF I don't like to put any kind of technology in a lounge chair. We have enough technology. Why do we need it? Maybe lighting will be different because they're using micro-technology and digital technology to design it. Maybe wallpaper will be a projection on the wall. I don't know.

I designed the Papilio chairs with this wide, butterfly back, because you're either watching TV or using a tablet or PC when you sit in them. That's life. This is a chair for computing; this is a bed for watching TV. Nobody ever said that, but people are already using them for that. So that's my way of connecting technology and furniture.

MF So how do you go from designing a phone to designing a chair?

NF The chair has been in our lives for a long time and we don't want to ignore it, because we need it. Chairs are changing too. The process is still being improved. For this chair I focus more on the technology that is happening right now. But for this phone I have to read the future, because this is a product that we have never used before.

David Chipperfield
'Architecture is probably the most collaborative thing you can do outside of war'

The British architect curated the Venice Architecture Biennale in 2012. He talked about the importance of bringing architects down from their pedestals to discuss buildings in a way ordinary people can understand.

Marcus Fairs What is the architecture biennale, and what's your involvement in it this year?

David Chipperfield The Venice Architecture Biennale was stimulated by the preexistence of the art biennale, which has been around a longer time. Most countries have a national pavilion, which is the responsibility of each country to curate and select participants.

However, in the centre of this whole zoo is the main exhibition, which is the responsibility of the biennale's curator, and that occupies 350 or so metres of the Corderie of the Arsenale, the military basin where boats were built and ropes were made. The infrastructure has grown over the years to take up the territory around it and take on the central pavilion in the Giardini. The curator is responsible for the theme and then for inviting participants to take part under that theme.

MF As the curator, what is the theme you've chosen for this year?

DC My title is Common Ground. In the context of the architecture biennale, clearly it has a sort of double meaning. Interestingly we tend not to use it about physical things. It is something you hear on Radio 4 when someone says, 'I had a meeting with the Prime Minister this morning and we have common ground on this issue.' But clearly its origins were physical: that's my ground, that's your ground, that's common ground.

Why I like this title is because it talks about intellectual common ground – as in what ideas do we share, where can we meet – but also as a metaphor for the idea of public space, shared space. And that is something that really needs to be back on the agenda. As a society we are, at the moment, inspired by the financial collapse of things we thought were secure. I think it's inspired us all to think a bit more carefully about the relationship between us as individuals, our own trajectory and what we belong to socially as one might call a collective.

MF In the past, you've compared architects to perfume boxes at Duty Free: on a pedestal, singular and isolated. How are you going to try and avoid that at this year's biennale?

DC The whole idea of common ground is trying to get people off their pedestal and standing on the ground, which we all share. I know

Name
David Chipperfield
Occupation
Architect
Location
Italian Cultural Institute, London
Date
May 2012

architects who I'm fortunate enough to share the odd whisky
with in a bar, and as soon as we've had that first whisky we
all share the same ideas, the same predicaments and concerns.
But there's no place to articulate those ideas beyond the bar.
So I'd like to show that these talents are grounded in something
that connects them horizontally, which you could describe as
an architectural culture.

I want to give oxygen to an architectural culture and say we
are the children of our parents. We have been taught by somebody.
Those teachers taught us things that have informed us. We
are inspired by our colleagues, maybe only out of the corner
of our eye. Maybe we don't want to admit what another architect
or generation has taught us. But that idea of affiliation, of

Above
Wall House
by Anupama
Kundoo at the
2012 Venice
Architecture
Biennale

**David
Chipperfield**

acknowledging where ideas come from, I think, is a way to be more honest about our common position. Everybody shining their wares and putting them on a stand and saying, 'This is what I do, this is what somebody else does,' – it's breaking down those barriers.

MF You say the biennale will be about architecture culture, not about architects. How will you achieve this?

DC My ambition is clear and it has been reassuring to find that architects are willing to join that idea, even though they are a bit stumped. I'm not trying to suppress architects, but in a way the place is the thing. I want great actors, but it's the story I want to come out.

The cast is impressive and they're from all generations – from Rafael Moneo and Norman Foster, a generation of architects who are now in their seventies, down to kids, as I would call them, of 30 and 40. I think each architect is thinking about ways of representing either affinities that they have, inspirations they

'The idea of public space, shared space, is something that really needs to be back on the agenda'

have or projects they might do together as a collaboration, so it's a diverse attempt to demonstrate ideas. It hasn't started with image; it started with ideas.

MF So you've not said to the architects, 'Send us your latest model in a box.' You've said, 'See the theme that we've set. Do something new and specific to that theme.'

DC They're not allowed to send their project in a box; I'll send it straight back. I want their contribution to be contextualised by an idea, not by them saying, 'This is my work, this is who I am.' There are people showing projects, but the reason the projects are there is because they're contextualised.

I'm not out to teach anybody anything. I'm fronting up to the fact that architecture is probably, as a peacetime activity, the most collaborative thing you can do outside of war. It's a thing that galvanises and draws upon resources, participation, collaboration. I can't think of anything that requires so much buy-in from the general public. I think that's an issue we have to articulate better, because the dialogue is predetermined by where we sit within society. If we isolate ourselves and if we're regarded with suspicion, society won't trust us and we won't engage society.

Good architecture is born of collaboration. If there's an agenda, that's what it is. It's not written above the door, but clearly I want us to come clean, to say – intellectually, physically and even in our built environment – that we're part of something more collaborative than anything else. Therefore let's look at our potential.

MF You've also said that architects don't have much common ground between themselves and the public. Could you elaborate on why that might be?

DC I don't think we've got good methods of talking about the diverse concerns that make a building happen. In the UK 'planning' is now called 'development control', as if it's someone with a chair and a whip trying to stop this animal escaping. It's sort of a negative idea of architecture.

By the way, I don't blame it for being like that. As architects, we sit on both sides of the table. We are just as furious about bad buildings and we say, 'Why the hell did that project ever get built?' But the level of discussion, dialogue and confrontation that seems to exist – you can see it coming and it just dooms the process.

If you do a museum, you've got a very informed board of trustees, a director, a budget that is sort of reasonable. There's a clear desire to do the building. But what about social housing? What about office buildings? What about normal architecture where people have not assembled themselves around finding good architects? What about 99.9 percent of the world? I think it's easy to have a dialogue about a museum with an informed board of trustees. How do you go out there and have a discussion about other things? That's more difficult.

MF We've been living in an era of the superstar architect and the iconic project. But your office has been working on more gentle, historically contextual work. How do you see today's architecture, and do you think we're moving away from that kind of star system?

DC We've always had icons. From my office I can see the Palace of Westminster and Big Ben. What a funny building, but how glad one is that it's there. And if it was rational and wasn't so fanciful, it wouldn't be half of what it is. I think we need icons. Does everything need to be turned into an icon? Does an extension on someone's house need to become an icon? Not that I don't think it's appropriate, but it becomes slightly irrelevant to the rest of the architectural debate.

If what we are doing becomes bespoke and architecture only becomes those special monuments, we become urban decorators. That's my issue of architecture that becomes self-referential: while it might be a beautiful museum or opera house, has it given any clue how other issues might be dealt with?

Janne Kyttanen
'Wasn't the web going to kill paper? I don't think anything will replace anything – it's just new technology'

A decade ago the Dutch designer was one of the first to prove that 3D printing could create beautiful, desirable products. He describes his vision for this fast-emerging technology and what it means for manufacturing.

Marcus Fairs Tell us about what's happened to you and what's happened to 3D manufacturing and 3D printing in the decade since you launched Freedom Of Creation.

Name
Janne Kyttanen
Occupation
Industrial
designer
Company
Freedom Of
Creation/3D
Systems
Location
3D Printshow,
London
Date
October 2012

Janne Kyttanen Well, at the time I started in 3D printing everything was very, very expensive, so it was extremely difficult to get the whole thing going. My dream was always to start an industry instead of designing individual products. So I think the first five, six or seven years were difficult both financially and in terms of having people believe in the vision. Only in the past three years have things started moving forward exponentially, into the industry I'd always envisioned. And especially in the last year. It's going great now.

MF Why has it suddenly taken off in the past few years?

JK There are some patents that have expired. And, of course, a massive awareness of the whole story. And, to be honest, the pricing has come down. You can print normal household products. Let's say an iPod Nano holder – it costs two euros to make. So, you know, why go buy something when you could just make your own?

MF You've just mentioned the expiring patents. Do you mean that companies that had held the patents for this manufacturing technology were preventing it from being widely taken up?

JK Well, I will say they weren't preventing anything, but of course that happens in any technology. Once some restrictions are taken off, the bigger crowd starts to flourish, and that's what I always believed in.

MF Freedom Of Creation is now owned by 3D Systems, so tell us more about that merger and about the company you're now working for.

JK That happened about a year and a half ago. We'd been talking for a number of years, about how I had always envisioned that the consumer world would be the final frontier for this type of adventure. What I needed was the technology, the software, the finance and a whole bunch of people running in the same direction. So they had that something I needed. And I had 12 years' worth of valuable content that we could quickly get going – instead of them having to hire in other designers or invest in another company to get it going. So for me it was a match made in heaven.

MF And they're a company that makes 3D printers?

JK Yeah. 3D Systems was started 25 years ago by Chuck Hull. His company invented the technology and the industry and invented the process of stereolithography[1]. From that, we've gotten pretty

1 Stereolithography is a 3D-printing process in which liquid resin is hardened by an ultraviolet laser

'You can print normal household products, so why go and buy something when you could just make your own?'

much all the 3D print platforms. And our latest venture is on a bigger scale altogether. It's going into the consumer market, going in with the Cube.

MF And the Cube is what?

JK It's an extrusion machine with a heated nozzle that makes things in 3D. It's very simple.

MF And this is aimed at the consumer market?

JK Yes. It's an entry-level machine for anybody to buy for the home.

MF Where is this kind of technology taking manufacturing, taking the design world? A lot of people are saying, 'This spells the end of the big manufacturing cycle of the mega-brands and mega-corporations.' But is it? Or is it just a bit of fun?

JK Wasn't the web going to be the killer for paper? And so forth? I don't think anything will replace anything. It's just that a massive 3D-manufacturing industry will also grow, I believe. These are just some new technologies, just a new thing.

Paul Priestman
'Boutique hotels annoy me. You walk in and trip over the rug'

The co-founder of design consultancy Priestmangoode spoke to us about his work on trains, planes and ships, and how it led to a radical design for a hospital ward.

Marcus Fairs Why is Priestmangoode based in London?

Paul Priestman All our clients come from overseas. We don't have any UK clients. But being in London means we can attract some of the best designers in the world. Most of the designers come from different countries, and a mixture of men and women, which is important. And I've always thought it was important to be in the centre of the city, if you're going to be in the city. We have about 30 designers at the moment and we're all based here, in Marylebone.

MF You're best known for trains and planes but you've also done hotels and other interior projects recently.

PP Our movement into hotels came from our work in transportation, which involves designing small private spaces in large public spaces. These small spaces have to be everything from a workspace to a sleeping space to a TV lounge, so they're very complex. We were the lead interior consultants on Heathrow Terminal 5, working with the architect Richard Rogers. We thought, 'Wouldn't it be interesting to apply that to hotels, to a fixed environment?' We started working on a hotel concept, a small luxury room in a small hotel. Applying this understanding to budget hotels, we've been working with Etap and Motel 6 in the States, and that's one of the cheapest budget hotel chains in the world.

MF What about interiors for vehicles?

PP We call them 'moving environments' as opposed to fixed environments. More recently we've designed a new range of cabins for Norwegian Cruise Line. It was a rewarding project because they asked us to tackle one of the most problematic areas in a cruise ship: the cabins at the centre, down below, with no view. We tackled that with compact rooms looking to attract a younger age group.

MF Interior design is often seen as architecture's poor relation. What's your view on that?

PP When we started working on hotel interiors, we started with the room first, because I don't believe what a hotel looks like on the outside is that important to you. Particularly on a business trip. What's important is: is the bed comfortable, what's the bathroom like? So we've designed the room first and the hotel around that room. That's very different to architecture.

MF So for you, interiors are about more than choosing furnishings?

PP The way we've approached hotel design is all bespoke. We've rolled out hotel rooms in 50,000 quantities. It's like product design. It's

Name
Paul Priestman
Occupation
Designer
Company
Priestmangoode
Location
His studio,
London
Date
June 2011

like car production. We approach it in a completely different way to designers and architects. We think about the practicalities.

When you design interiors for an aircraft, if a part becomes broken, the aircraft might not take off. It has to be designed for a purpose. If not, it's just not acceptable. It infuriates me in some hotels, when you sit in bed and you can't read a book because the light wasn't designed correctly. That would be unacceptable in an aircraft, so we apply our aircraft design to hotels. Design has evolved from being airy fairy, where it looks nice but doesn't work.

MF Many interiors are overdesigned.

PP One thing that really annoys me is what they call boutique hotels. You walk in and trip over the rug. When you design a shower, the tap should be in a place where you don't get wet when you turn it on. I mean, how many hotels do you go into and you have to get wet to just move the knob? That gives design a bad name.

Lighting is terrible. Not being able to switch off all the lights when you're in bed. The amount of hotels I stay in where you get into bed and find the light on, then have to switch on all the lights to find out why it's not working. As an interior designer of aircraft, ships and planes, this is not acceptable. I do think the big hotel brands are waking up to this. They've become more professional.

MF So you start with the interior and then moving on to the architecture, rather than the other way around?

PP With the hotels we're doing, the clients have initially asked us to design the rooms, then the public spaces, corridors and reception areas and now the whole hotel, including the exterior. We are, in effect, designing the whole building – from the customer's perspective, rather than what it looks like from the outside. Of course that's something we work very hard to get right, but it's not the starting point. Many hoteliers will tell you the most important things are the bed and bathroom. You get those right first, those are the things people will remember and come back to.

MF What are travellers looking for today?

PP One of the trends in hotels at the moment is high quality at a lower price. So we've been enabling business travellers staying at a low-cost hotel to have the same quality of a more expensive hotel. I think there's a move away from hotels offering concierge service: carry your bags, check in, all the bits a business traveller wouldn't necessarily need. What they're concentrating on is the quality of the room and the amenities within that. Sometimes a hotel will expect the guest to eat elsewhere, so there's a slight move away from destination hotels to service-orientated experiences.

MF What are the trends in plane or train interiors?

PP One of the trends in aircraft design is a move away from the interior looking like a plane. It frustrates me that you board this amazing flying machine, which is beautifully detailed on the outside, and inside there are floppy bits of plastic and squeaky

Paul Priestman

fittings. What we're approaching now, what a lot of airlines are doing is placing furniture within this beautiful object – not trying to make it look like part of the aircraft so much as a floating space. Certainly in first class, we're moving away from closed cabins, which feedback shows people feel a bit nervous about, into a more open hotel-lounge feel. On take-off or landing you press a button and the walls come up to give you privacy. It's evolving quickly and flexibility is key. And reducing weight, because weight means fuel and we're trying to make the process more efficient.

MF You designed a hospital ward. Tell us about that.

PP We embarked on a hospital project from our learning of aircraft. There are some amazing similarities between the way an aircraft has to function, for safety reasons, and how a hospital could function – particularly now that many treatments are done in the day and you don't have to stay overnight. So we came up with this idea of a recovery lounge, a series of small, semi-enclosed spaces with chairs in them. You have a bit of privacy when you're recovering and a bit drowsy, but you still get the level of care of an overnight patient and you don't feel isolated. The idea is you can save money and make the experience better.

MF Was that a self-initiated project?

PP Yes, it was. The idea was to push this information out into the world and see what responses we get back. This is our way of being able to leapfrog from one discipline to another, a rather happy accident. We first started designing trains because Richard Branson called us up and said, 'You haven't designed a train. Do you want to design a train?' But why should we rely on someone forcing it? Why don't we actually push that ourselves?

MF You've been doing a lot of business in China.

PP We're designing high-speed trains for the Chinese mainland. We're part-way through an eight-year contract with a railway manufacturer in China and we're designing high-speed trains in North America, South America, Australasia and the Middle East. But I've been learning so much from the Chinese. So often people ask, 'Aren't you worried about them taking your ideas?' It's completely the opposite, actually. I think we have a lot to learn from their work ethic and their teamworking, which is different from the European way, and so fast.

MF You don't have a house style. Why not?

PP It allows us to work with a lot of different brands in the same sector. With airlines, we can be working with four or five companies, for whom we produce completely different worlds. Our infrastructure for countries becomes part of those countries. High-speed trains are the modern iconic vision of a country, like the bullet train that runs in front of Mount Fuji. We bring those cultural elements to the things we're designing. Certainly the work we're doing with the Chinese is all about iconic imagery,

understanding the culture to make sure everything is applicable for that country.

MF So China is investing in high-speed rail partly for branding?

PP When we're designing a train, the head, face and look are critical. It's got to be smooth and slithery to go at high speeds. But we're also trying to think about where that country might like to be in five or ten years' time and project that imagery onto the object so it's taking the country forward rather than backwards.

MF You've remarked that design is a business, not about having fun.

PP Design without money isn't design. Design is one tool that allows our clients to make money. It allows them to move into new areas or become stronger within their sector. It's amazingly satisfying to design something that's successful and carries on for years.

Above
Visualisation of a proposed high-speed train interior by Priestmangoode

Sou Fujimoto

'The grid is straight and artificial, but if you have a lot of it, it becomes organic and cloud-like'

The Japanese architect discussed the opposing concepts of nature and architecture and explained how his design for the Serpentine Gallery Pavilion tried to fuse the two.

Name
Sou Fujimoto
Occupation
Architect
Location
Serpentine
Gallery Pavilion,
London
Date
June 2013

Ben Hobson Tell us the story behind the pavilion.

Sou Fujimoto The inspiration started with these beautiful surroundings. I came to Kensington Gardens last November and I was so impressed by the beautiful green surroundings. So I tried to create in this green environment something between nature and architecture. I tried to create transparent structures that melt into the background of green – at times standing out but other times melting into the background. But that was a starting point.

Then I was thinking, 'This spot could be a nice café,' and 'This could be good for a performance and events space,' so I tried to provide a diverse space where people could choose to sit on it or to climb up it or something like that – so it would be like an artificial landscape.

And how to realise such a landscape? We found a way to do this grid. Because it is quite transparent, we could make it like part of the organic landscape. We realised that the contrast between this artificial, ordered grid and the organic experience is another mixture of the architectural and the natural order. So I would say the main concept is the space between nature and architecture – in the experience itself or in the sense of order. It is the creation of a duality.

BH It's interesting that you describe the pavilion as a landscape rather than as a building. What is the relationship between architecture and nature, exactly? Because this occurs in a lot of your work.

SF The relationship between architecture and nature is a fundamental topic that architects have been thinking about in history. In Japan, in our culture, we have a long tradition of treating nature and architecture or artificial things equally and integrating the two things together. So I am interested in how our living environment is going to be in the future. This idea of considering architecture and nature is really important for the future, I feel.

In my previous projects, that kind of interest in nature and architecture has been an undercurrent, a very important undercurrent. It is always underlining the projects in our office.

BH In your press conference you described the pavilion as a cloud-like structure. But you have used a very rigid geometric grid to achieve that form.

SF The idea of the grid came to us in the process. I found out it could be nice to have a transparency to the grid – and the space within the grid is quite small, 40 centimetres and 80 centimetres, so it means a huge amount of the grid is creating the atmosphere. I felt that the grid itself is quite straight and quite artificial, but if you have a huge amount of repetition in the grid, then it becomes more like an organic, cloud-like, forest-like, tree-like atmosphere. I was fascinated by such a contrast between the sharp, artificial white grids and the organic, formless experience. So I tried to find out what it is and tried to challenge the possibilities.

Above
Sou Fujimoto's
2013 Serpentine
Gallery Pavilion

Sou Fujimoto

BH How did you arrange the lattice to create this organic form?

SF Some areas are less dense and some are really dense. The area behind me is a dense area, which has more strength; it's translucent to almost opaque, like a wall. The less dense area is more transparent.

If you come to an opaque area, you feel more protected and cosy, and if you are closer to the transparent area, it's more open and surrounded by trees and green, and some areas are even open to the sky. Even the roof itself has a diversity of density, so you can see a shadow of the trees, a shadow under the forest – an organic situation is happening. For me, it's amazing to see how these straight grids could create such a rich experience inside.

BH How do you keep the rain out?

SF The whole structure is made of grids, so to think about how to block the rain – of course we couldn't put a roof on the structure because it would spoil the beauty from below. We tried to find a way to put up a roof between the structures. And then, finally, we found the idea to use this transparent polycarbonate with these round-shaped discs overlapping one another to keep out

'In Japan, we have a long tradition of treating nature and architecture equally and integrating the two things together'

the rain. And then finally, yesterday, I found out that – and this was kind of beyond my imagination – that each polycarbonate tile reflects the water from the rain and sometimes if there is wind coming, it starts to swing in a beautiful contrast with the grid.

BH You are still only 40, which makes you the youngest architect to be invited to design the Serpentine Gallery Pavilion.

SF It was surprising and a great honour to hear about that. Actually, I didn't know much about being the youngest architect to design the Serpentine Gallery Pavilion before this. It was a big surprise. At the same time it is a big challenge and a big pressure. Of course, the pressure is not a negative pressure. I am a personality who can enjoy the whole situation. And this was a really precious thing.

BH You are actually the third Japanese architect to design the pavilion. What do you think it is about Japanese design that is popular with the Serpentine Gallery, and the UK in general?

SF Yes, I'm the third Japanese architect: Toyo Ito and SANAA and me. Toyo Ito and SANAA opened the door for Japanese architects into the world, I think. We are very lucky. Because of them, the world expects Japanese architecture to be something nice. So I would like to say thank you to the upper generations.

We have big pressure to do something different from them and something unique for us. Again, it's a nice challenge. And fortunately I am a good friend of Sejima-san and Nishizawa-san of SANAA and also Ito-san. I am doing something different from them and also it has a continuous stream of the Japanese architects' spirit, I think.

BH In the UK there is a continuing debate about internships – there has been a culture here for some time of people working for free. What's the view in Japan about internships?

SF In Japan, as well, we have a long history – from Toyo Ito and SANAA to our office – of interns, and usually the student works for free for several periods. In my office there are many interns, especially from abroad. They get a scholarship and come to my office and spend three months to six months there and they are really helpful and they are also really powerful.

In Japan we don't yet have much discussion about whether it is good or bad. I'm not sure. It's a nice opportunity for all of us – for the architects to know younger generations and for them to know how architects in Japan and the different countries are working. Because if you have to pay all the interns, then you have to limit the numbers of interns. We couldn't provide such opportunities for students or younger people in a real architecture office otherwise.

In Japan, the interns are making the models – they make beautiful models. If the internship is for a long period, for example longer than six months, they can join more deeply in the project. But for us, it's nice to make it more intense. But I understand the conversation about whether working for free is good or bad. I'd like to see the discussion continue.

Andy Millns

'When you can create a world from scratch, there's really no limit to what you can do with it'

We visited the London office of 3D production company Inition to hear the views of co-founder Andy Millns on the future of virtual and augmented reality.

Marcus Fairs What does Inition do?

Andy Millns Inition is a production company that specialises in harnessing emerging technologies such as augmented reality, virtual reality, 3D printing and 3D scanning. We produce installations for exhibitions, retail or events. We call it experiential.

MF I remember virtual reality from the 1990s and it was awful. How much further has all that technology come in the past years?

AM Virtual reality was the technology that set me off on this career path in the first place. I was absolutely obsessed by virtual reality in the '90s, every chance to use it, every magazine. But we were 20 years too early in terms of the hardware being mature enough and the software platforms being there. So now it's exciting that, 20 years later, finally the hardware has got to a point where the experience matches people's expectations.

MF What is virtual reality?

AM Virtual reality is where we use interface devices to create a sense of presence in a digital world. The most obvious of these is the head-mounted digital display, such as an Oculus Rift headset. It straps on to your head but also has a tracking device in it, so it knows which way you're looking, so it can simulate from different angles.

MF What is this used for, generally?

AM I think virtual reality is the most versatile interface possible. It can simulate any number of worlds, whether they're realistic or complete abstract fantasy. It has a huge number of applications. When you can create a world from scratch, there's really no limit to what you can do with it.

MF How do you see this technology becoming more mainstream?

AM I think this mirrors other technologies like 3D printing. 3D printing has been around for a while, used by a very small number of designers. It's the same with virtual reality. Virtual reality has been around for a while, there have been a lot of research labs. But now there are thousands more people with a virtual-reality headset than there were even a year ago, so we're seeing a huge explosion in the application. The applications are just blossoming day by day.

Name
Andy Millns
Company
Inition
Location
His studio,
London
Date
January 2014

MF Could architects use virtual reality?

AM One of the great things about virtual reality is it provides a very realistic 3D sense of the world. We've all seen 3D cinema and TV, but they can't actually represent distances or sizes. When you've got a head-mounted display you can guarantee that the stereo experience, the 3D experience, will be the same as the real world. I can make a wall appear three metres away or even a metre from your face or maybe an object right in front of your face, so you get a really accurate sense of the scale of places. It's very useful, for example, for architects or car designers who are trying to portray something on a realistic scale.

MF How might an architect or a car designer use that?

AM They can plug it into existing CAD packages to use in the office. Once that's been done, it's viewed on screen in full 3D or on a virtual-reality headset.

MF So people can walk around a car or a building that isn't actually there?

AM Yes, with a headset. The one thing that's missing with the Oculus Rift headset is the ability to track positions. At the moment it's just using a tilting-type sensor that can tell you what direction you're looking in, but it doesn't give you an accurate position. That's the next big add-on that will need to be cracked to allow this sort of application.

MF Would that be something like GPS technology?

AM Yes. Tracking systems such as GPS give you a very low accuracy tracking. But to do something like walk around a car or a building, we actually need millimetre-type tracking and a very low-type latency, so it gives very quick position information. If there's any sort of lag between your actual movement and the virtual world movement, it can create nausea.

MF Once that tracking has been figured out, what then becomes possible?

AM The sort of tracking we need to do, accurate position tracking, is available already and we have an example here of a system that does that by using infrared cameras and shiny marker balls. The problem is that it's still priced in the tens of thousands of pounds, so for that to get into homes, we need a slightly different approach.

MF When you talk about getting this into homes, would that be for entertainment purposes?

AM We still don't know how people would react with virtual worlds at home, especially on the gaming side – whether you'll still be sat down or whether there will be some sort of device where you're stood up and actually simulating walking. But certainly gaming is going to make a big impact this year.

Entertainment in the home is going to be a huge application for virtual reality. I also see it being a logical next step for feature films, for narratives, as a way of telling stories by filming in

360 degrees. There haven't been any high-production examples of 360-degree narratives yet, but we will probably see that happening in 2014.

MF The Oculus Rift headset has been getting a lot of press recently.

AM Oculus Rift has been the poster child for virtual reality. It has certainly brought virtual reality back into the public spotlight. It's actually very simple display technology, enabled by the fact that we now have high-resolution screens of a particular size, thanks to smartphones.

The actual design is similar to what we had in Victorian viewers 100 years ago – it's two simple lenses, and rather than having two pieces of cardboard we now have digital screens. The tracking device that allows you to see what direction you're looking in is the same device that we have in our smartphones now. It allows you to sense tilt angle. So it's actually a very simple device. There are no patents on it and it's only a couple of hundred pounds, so we're seeing a huge explosion in the number of those devices. And they will get higher resolution, more lightweight and give an even wider field of view.

MF Isn't there a new version out that is high definition?

AM There is a new version out, yes. The Oculus Rift headset itself is actually very low resolution. You're getting a less than standard-definition picture in each eye. And it's a very big picture, so when people look at it, it seems quite grainy. It's actually quite a trivial

> ‘I can make a wall
> appear a metre
> from your face or an
> object right in front
> of your face, so
> you get a really
> accurate sense of
> the scale of place’

upgrade to put even a 2K panel in, or a 4K, like we're seeing in some consumer TVs. That will transform the experience and give you something akin to an HD TV.

MF Will people start wearing these headsets to go shopping? Will the real and virtual blur in that sense? Or is Oculus Rift always going to be something you put on to escape from reality?

AM There are two strains of headsets we're seeing now. The Google Glass-style headset, where the primary design objective is to be lightweight and unobtrusive, which only gives you a small

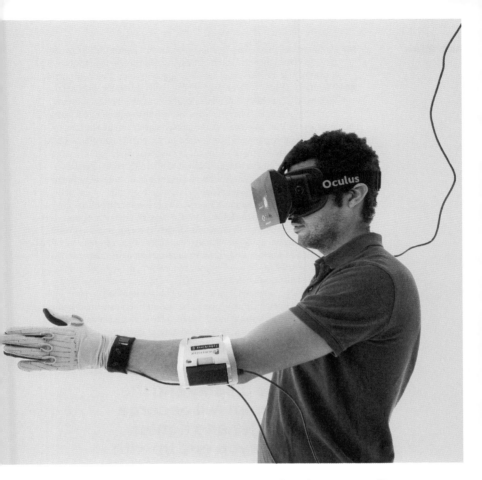

image in the corner of your field of view. Then we'll see the
Oculus Rift type of headset, which is designed to replace your
entire world and give you a higher resolution, the biggest picture
possible. Eventually the two will converge. It'll be some sort
of contact lens, it will go in your eye and it will give you all those
things: a huge image, high resolution and also the ability to mix
images with the real world.

MF Is the contact lens idea something you've just thought of, or are
people actively working on it?

AM There are wearable head-mount displays that do involve a contact
lens, but we don't know which technology will win in the end.
There are devices that shine a laser light directly onto your retina.
There's so much activity in this area.

Above
A demonstration
of an Oculus Rift
virtual-reality
headset

175

Andy Millns

MF We're almost stepping into cyborg territory when it's on your eye. Do you think in the future that the idea of a cyborg will become a reality? Is the future of technology integrated with the body?

AM The inevitable future of these things is that the display and the human will become tighter and tighter, until you end up with a cyborg scenario, where you have something embedded inside your brain that has a direct interface to your visual cortex.

At the moment, all the devices rely on projecting light right into your eyes. A much more successful way of doing this would be to bypass the eye altogether and directly interface with the brain. We're already seeing things like this on the hearing side with cochlear implants.

MF So that would merge artificial and real vision. What next?

AM This interfacing would deal with the sound, then the vision. The next step would be a WiFi or Bluetooth-type interface in your brain to augment the processing capacity of your brain.

MF You've just done a project with fashion designer Gareth Pugh in Selfridges.

AM That installation is a virtual-reality experience of travelling through the world of Gareth Pugh. You walk into the store, put the headset on and you're immersed in a three-minute experience of his world. It's almost like a music video, in this abstract world. There's a soundtrack. The visuals are tightly connected to the sound. We're playing with ideas of space, because you can really accurately present a 3D space in this world. We can play with the

'The display and the human will become tighter and tighter, until you end up with a cyborg scenario'

idea of being in a confined space, that space enlarging or breaking out, having things almost flying towards you, making you feel almost in jeopardy. There are also sensations of flying, which can be reproduced with virtual reality.

MF For fashion shows in the future, instead of fashion journalists flying out to New York, could you send them a headset or a USB stick and they could experience it from home?

AM Virtual reality is so versatile, it could replace all sorts of things. It could replace something mundane from your desktop, your PC screen, to replacing an entire fashion show and putting you right inside of it. But it can also create experiences that have not even yet been conceived in the real world.

AM In future the possible scenarios could be to have a seat by the side of the runway, based on live-action 360-degree filming, which is another area virtual reality enables. Once you film in 360, you allow the viewer to view any angle from a position.

Another possibility is to use 360-degree camera technology to give a live-action impression of being somewhere. That can be done live or afterwards. You can put someone in any position in a catwalk show and allow them to look around as if they were there. This idea of putting another person in a place live is known as 'telepresence'. By using the vision and sound queues, you can make someone feel as if they're seeing it live.

MF So let's use the example of the fashion show.

AM We can put several or even thousands of people in a seat by the side of a runway and they can actually experience what it's like to be there. This is enabled not only by virtual-reality headsets but by 360-degree camera technology, and we're seeing a huge amount of activity in the area of 360-degree cameras. Ricoh has just released a 360-degree stills camera. There are prosumer and professional 360-degree cameras coming up to market that will enable this type of activity.

MF What do you mean by a 360-degree camera?

AM A 360-degree camera films in every direction from a single perspective. It's almost like a ball with cameras pointing in each direction. Some are very small, so you can mount them on people's heads or put them on quadrocopters to give a 360-degree impression. Once you've captured a 360-degree image from a 360-degree camera, it can be sent out via the web and people can view it using a headset. Each person can look in any direction.

MF Inition also works with augmented reality. How does that work?

AM Augmented reality is the idea of bringing in extra information and layering in onto the real world. You could do this with a tablet. We're using a camera on a tablet to bring in a real-world picture and layering images and objects as if they were there in real life.

MF You created an augmented architectural model with architect Zaha Hadid. Can you explain how that works?

AM We made a scale model of one of her buildings. Then we created an iPad app that layered on extra information like air flow and landscaping to bring this model to life using augmented reality.

We could also use the iPad to reveal the underlying structure of the building and the various services inside the building. We could also look at the different lighting effects – how the light looked at night, how the shadows looked at various times of day.

MF How could this technology help architects?

AM Augmented reality provides a very intuitive way of viewing 3D data on top of a real-world model. The navigation, for example,

Andy Millns

If I've got an iPad and augmented-reality app, in order to look closer I simply move in closer. To look from different perspectives I simply move around. It gives you a very powerful impression of how that design will look.

MF So future architects could be using this technology to quickly show clients various options?

AM Yes. For design review it's a very powerful tool because everyone can be given an iPad. One person can lead the presentation so all the iPads are synced. If they wanted to show all the services in a building, they would select that and everyone would see the same view, but from their own perspective.

MF Why aren't architects using it now?

AM This is really because the tools haven't been fully integrated into their design tools. At the moment we're seeing augmented reality used for high-end presentations or even on the sales and marketing side, which is where most of our work is.

MF You've worked with developers and estate agents. How is it used in that area?

AM We've worked with property developers on the marketing side to bring properties to life using augmented reality. Some of the advantages are that we can bring an animated model to life. We can also show live availability, so you can look at the model and select what type of apartment you're interested in. It will show you live data and which ones are still on the market.

MF How will this become part of our daily lives, where using a device such as a tablet isn't really practical?

AM I think using tablets out and about in a city environment is not something that was ever going to take off, standing in the street and holding up a tablet. When we can track natural features in the city and have devices that are sat in your eye, and it's not obvious you're wearing them, that's when augmented reality will really take off – when we can get all sorts of information layered onto the urban view.

MF Does that mean augmented realities and virtual realities will converge in the future?

AM Yes, I think augmented and virtual realities will essentially merge into the same thing. We'll have devices that can either completely replace the real world with a virtual environment or mix the two for augmented reality.

MF Do you think virtual reality is the more exciting one?

AM Certainly at the moment, with the current display technology, I think virtual reality offers exciting possibilities for immersive experiences. There's only so far you can go with a tablet.

MF Do you think virtual reality is this year's biggest technology?

AM I think there's a lot of interest in display devices that we've worked with over the years, but virtual reality is the interface. There really isn't anything beyond that, once you can create someone's

world from scratch. At the moment we've got an extremely low-resolution device out there, which 10,000 or 20,000 developers are using. In the next year or two, we're going to see a device where it's almost impossible to distinguish reality, when we get to resolutions such as 4K display.

MF Will we see that because people are working on it? Or is that just a prediction?

AM I think the display technology is there. The headset design is very simple, so it's a very easy step to get from what we've got now to a very high-end device. It's going to happen very quickly. When we start to get very high-resolution headsets, with the type of display technology we're seeing on the market now, it's going to blur that line between the virtual and the real.

Above
Demonstration of Inition's augmented-reality iPad app

Konstantin Grcic

'I'm putting objects on plinths like pieces of art, so visitors can really see them'

We met the industrial designer at his Design Real exhibition at London's Serpentine Gallery. He explained why he chose to display everyday objects as if they were works of art.

Rose Etherington What was your role in pulling together this show?

Konstantin Grcic I was asked to curate this show of 43 products made by the design industry today, things that are in production, and things that are very different but somehow all relevant and significant to our lives.

RE The exhibition includes objects that have been designed for the domestic environment alongside tools for industry.

KG I wanted to create a larger picture of what products are and explain the complexity of our world of products. So it's a bird's-eye view of everything the design industry is creating. But in order to make that, you have other products: a machine, a robot. In order to ship the product from factory to warehouse, you have trucks and trains and containers. In order to package the products, you have the packaging and so on. You have the diversity of products I'm showing here, which tries to speak about all these aspects.

Some of the products that are closer to our lives are the things we live with, domestic products. But others are part of the chain, or they are related to it because of how they are made. I think that's a fascinating point of view and a relevant one for understanding the complexity of industry, the knowledge to find better solutions and also to feel more comfortable about our environment.

RE The products have been displayed in quite an unusual way for a design show.

KG The gallery is a museum, it is an art space. Showing design in such a context means a certain form of liberty. I don't need to do a real design show, a show like in a design museum, where next to the product a board of text says what it is, how it's made and so on. I think the fine arts are displayed in another way, leaving away comment and exposing things in a way that is much more open to interpretation. This is a beautiful form of viewing things. You're actually looking at something rather than being told what you're looking at and why.

In one part of the exhibition, I'm putting the objects on plinths. I'm hanging them on the wall. I'm treating them as sculptures, as pieces of art. And I'm leaving them completely uncommented, celebrating their creation and their beauty. That means the visitor is encouraged to really see them.

Name
Konstantin Grcic
Occupation
Industrial
designer
Location
Serpentine
Gallery, London
Date
November 2009

But taking away the information altogether would be too simple. I'm not saying these things are sculptures. I wanted simply to separate the information. The stories about the products are in a different space, the central space. It was important for me to provide the information but separate it from the product.

As part of the whole project we've created a website, a database, something like Wikipedia, a vessel or repository of information about each one of these objects, the most direct type of information about how it's made, who designed it, what it is for. But then this information goes into more lateral thinking, what this relates to or where it comes from and other things that relate to it. I think this should be part of our culture, to see products this way, to understand the world that way, that everything relates to

Above
Products mounted on plinths for Konstantin Grcic's 2009 Serpentine Gallery show

Konstantin Grcic

everything and there are much broader stories behind the products that decode the complexity of our environment.

RE You've chosen to display products by famous designers like Zaha Hadid alongside designs by anonymous people.

KG Curating the show, I was very conscious that my selection should not create any kind of dogma about what design is. I'm giving examples. I want to show the beauty, the complexity, the diversity of what design is and where we find design and where industry produces these objects. But I never want to say, 'This is good design,' which means it excludes all the other things I would indirectly say are not good design.

The diversity would be that I would include a pair of shoes by Zaha Hadid next to a flight container designed by, well, we don't know. I'm showing very technical, engineered things next to very

'My selection should not create any kind of dogma about what design is. I want to show the beauty, the complexity, the diversity of design'

basic products. I'm showing things you know and recognise and I'm showing you things you may have never seen close up.

I should point out also that design is about aesthetics and form and material qualities, even signature and style. I think, even in that respect, the exhibition shows many different possibilities and interpretations. It's not saying only the simple things are right. There are some very complicated forms next to extremely simple forms. There are expensive mouldings next to low-tech products. There are signature pieces next to anonymous ones. And there are things made in high volume next to pieces made by an industry so specialised that they only make 50 or 100 per year.

RE You are a designer. How have you approached this project, which is essentially curation?

KG Being a designer means that you naturally think about design all the time – not only your own projects but all the things around you. From my own working experience I've seen the factory floor, I've seen the warehouses, I have some understanding of the logistics, the difficulties, the constraints, where the opportunities are in industry, and I find that extremely fascinating. So the invitation to curate such a show is an invitation to expand on my own knowledge and to formulate my own statement about all these things I know, what I feel is really significant and how I can tell that story in the form of an exhibition.

I think exhibitions are a beautiful form of communication. They are really about experience. It's incredible to show these things in front of you, just their physical impact. Maybe a chair you see in the context of such a show, you view it in a different way.

RE What is your favourite object in the exhibition?

KG I don't think there is a favourite object in the exhibition for me. The exhibition works on this number: 43 things together and their relationship. The 43 things are so different in their material, their form, what they do, where they come from, their significance to our lives: that creates the picture I was interested in. I like every single piece, but it's not like I want to have any one of them stand out and be more significant than the others.

James Dyson
'Things always go wrong, every day. But following your product down a production line is thrilling'

The British designer and inventor explained why sketching is so central to the design process and discussed his inspirations for new products, such as the bladeless fan he launched in 2010.

Name
James Dyson
Occupation
Industrial
designer
and inventor
Company
Dyson
Location
Dyson
showroom,
London
Date
June 2010

Marcus Fairs How do you decide which problems to tackle? Is it your personal experience of being frustrated with things?

James Dyson We choose products that we have a personal problem with. We chose to tackle the hand dryer because, going to use those hot-air dryers, you give up and wipe your hands on your trousers and your hands feel chapped. What they're trying to do is turn the energy into steam and it's very energy-consuming and takes a long time. We launch that frustration in our brains and develop technology to try and solve it. And sometimes we think of a better idea when we're developing that technology or we come across something that works far better than the thing we were trying to use it for. So the important thing is to be always experimenting, building prototypes, trying to develop new technology.

The Airblade hand dryer came out of a product we hadn't yet launched. We were experimenting with air-knife technology and suddenly noticed how well it dried your hands. We realised you didn't need heat; you could just scrape the water off your hands like a windscreen wiper. Sometimes you just come across something by accident and you've got a product and you've got the fun of developing that product from the technology of that idea.

MF What's the typical design process at Dyson? Does it start with sketching, or with engineering?

JD You may observe a technology through building prototypes and testing things or you may set out to develop a new technology like we did with our electric motors, for example. Very often that involves sketching at an early stage, then you go into the workshop or machine shop and test things. Then, as you're developing the technology, you try to realise the product you're trying to make with it. Absolutely we sketch, and we communicate to one another with words as engineers, but sketching is a powerful way of doing it. That's why my pencil is my favourite object, because it's how I express myself and how all our engineers express themselves. Drawing is very important and the best engineers are always very good at drawing.

MF You talk about design and engineering. What's the difference?

JD I started off at the Royal College of Art in 1966. I started as a designer because I had studied classics at school, so the idea of being an engineer – I didn't understand that at all. But as I started doing design, I realised engineering was more important, really. I was actually doing architecture at the time, and I realised that in the future the engineering of the building was going to express the performance of the building and how it looked. I suddenly discovered that I was interested in engineering. And so it is with products that the engineering and the technology are actually more important than how it looks.

The reason I said that is if something looks wonderful and performs badly, you really fall out of love with it. But if something looks awful but works really well, I don't say you fall totally in love with it, but you enjoy using it. I always think a Blackberry mobile phone is quite a good example. A Blackberry is a wonderful thing to use but it looks awful. Nevertheless it's not totally horrible to use because it works well. So get the function right, how it works, then try and make it look exciting and interesting.

MF What's your view of the design scene today?

JD It's interesting because design courses at universities have really become engineering courses. What they used to call 'product design', which you might as well call 'styling', has almost disappeared. Styling, or product design, only became a profession in the 1930s with Harley Earl, the head of design at General Motors. In the Victorian era and the early twentieth century, engineers designed.

I think that in the twenty-first century we're swinging back to the designer. I think someone who is more of a designer than an engineer is often more capable of thinking of a product conceptually, so I think there's absolutely a place for someone who is more interested in what products are like to use or feel. They can often see the whole story better than an engineer, who is heavily involved in the technology. So I think the two can mix well and there's no reason why someone can't be both.

MF How did you become an inventor?

JD I went from the Royal College of Art to an engineering company to learn how to be an engineer. I decided that just designing the product wasn't enough for me. I wanted to design the technology and manufacture the product – not actually sell it but be involved with the people who used it. I wanted to be in that whole process. I didn't want anyone telling me what to design.

I may be a complete control freak, but then I love manufacturing. I love it because it's so difficult. Things always go wrong, every day. It's a very frustrating thing but the sight of a product that you develop and follow down a production line is thrilling.

The first product wasn't for my own company at all. It was for a public engineering company and I developed, engineered and designed a landing craft that the chairman had invented. It was a high-speed landing craft, so I learned the whole process of exporting it and sending it all around the world.

Then I decided to go off on my own and do the Ballbarrow – that's the wheelbarrow with a big red ball instead of a wheel – which I felt much happier doing because I use it myself. I didn't actually use landing craft. I mean, they're fun to use, but I wasn't a customer of landing craft. I was a customer of the wheelbarrow, so it was great fun being a designer and actually making something that people use at home every day. But it wasn't a commercial success.

While I was doing it, I saw a bit of technology to overcome a really irritating problem that frustrated me: the home vacuum cleaner. The technology actually came from some production equipment we had, from the paint-spray equipment used to paint the frames. I came across the idea of using cyclones in vacuum cleaners to collect dust, because the bag clogs. It's always

'We choose products we have a personal problem with. We launch that frustration in our brains and develop technology to try and solve it'

a wonderful way to start, a frustration with something. So I set about developing it. It took five years and 5500 prototypes and I was heavily in debt and really thought I ought to licence it rather than borrow millions of pounds to set it up. So I went off to try and licence it to manufacturers and failed. I wasted five or six years doing that.

Eventually I decided I should produce it myself, even though everybody said, 'Don't be mad, you're not a businessman.' So I went off to borrow a million pounds and did it and it worked. Gradually I've managed to build up a fantastic team of creative people, of scientists and engineers. We have great fun all day long, solving problems, still finding frustrations and having lots of failures every day with our prototypes.

So it's still the same sort of work I've been doing for the past 40 years but it's on a much larger scale – and I'm getting to work with lots of people who are much more intelligent and creative than me.

MF You mentioned the Dyson vacuum cleaner, which is what you are most famous for. But what are you launching here today?

JD Today we're launching two new fans. We launched a desk fan about six months ago and we've now done what are called a tower and pedestal fan, which have a higher flow than our desk fan, which could be used at home but also in offices. They don't have blades and they deliver a much smoother stream of air flow. Blades chop air, so you feel this sort of buffeting effect. With our system of jetting air out of an annulus and drawing in air from behind it, you get a totally smooth air flow and, of course, the fans are easier to clean and are completely safe.

One of the things I find particularly annoying about pedestal fans is adjusting the height – you know, you have to undo a clamp at an angle. And that's made more difficult because the motor is up at the top in the middle of the fan blades, so all the weight is at the top. We've put our weight down at the bottom, so it's very stable. The air goes up the nice, fat aluminium tube into what we call the amplifier. The height is adjusted just by pushing it and it stays where you put it. That's because we've got a constant rate spring in there and it's only supporting this really light amplifier. So you don't have that awful business of undoing clamps, getting it to the right position, doing it up again, finding it falls a few degrees... It's remote controlled and the control sits on the top by the magnet, so you don't lose it. It fits the curvature.

MF Do you look around and think, 'This is so crazy. Products could be so much better'?

JD Oh no. I think the world is getting much better. And part of the reason for that is any country in the world can make anything now: China, India, Korea and Japan, even Iran. They're producing lots of engineers and scientists and they've realised there's a tremendous international trade competition, and to export anything to create wealth, you've got to have something that other people haven't got. You've got to have technology.

Most countries are developing technology at an astonishing rate. So I think products are fantastic now compared to what they were 40 years ago. Cars work – it's an absolute delight. Vacuum cleaners work. Think of bean-to-cup coffee machines. Everything works incredibly well now.

Richard Rogers
'The only technology in the old Lloyd's building was a Xerox machine. People were writing with quills and ink'

The architect spoke to us in depth about three of his most important projects: the Centre Pompidou, the Lloyd's building and his latest addition to the London skyline, the Leadenhall Building.

Marcus Fairs A major retrospective of your work is about to open at the Royal Academy. What does the show say about your life and your career?

Richard Rogers This is the first one-man show the Royal Academy has done on architecture. We've decided to call the exhibition Inside Out because I often put the structure and ducts on the outside of buildings, for functional as well as aesthetic reasons. But the real title is 'Ethos'. The idea is that we have a responsibility to answer the passer-by and society as a whole.

On the outside, visitors will see some yellow, green and blue ducts, as a sort of signature. They go up some steps to four spaces. The first space is really the 'ethos' room, bright pink, and on each wall is a different statement, a different concept, if you like. One wall says 'a place for all people, all ages, all creeds, the rich and the poor'. That was actually the first paragraph I wrote with Renzo Piano when we entered the Pompidou competition, but it really shows the heart of the exhibition because it gave us a way of handling the Pompidou not just as a building but as a place, which I'm much more interested in.

On another wall is the Athenian oath, which is, 'We will leave this city not less but greater, better and more beautiful than it was left to us.' It's an oath that I would like to think we are all trying to keep, and uses beauty in that very broad, shall we say Greek, way – democratic and intellectual, not purely aesthetic.

Another wall explains what ethos means to me and how I work, in a way. I work very much with colleagues, with friends. Architecture is about teams. The idea that you suddenly wake up and do a sketch is not true. If anything, when I do that I usually wake up with a hangover the next morning, because it never works like that. You do it piece by piece. I often quote the chairman of Lloyd's, who, when I was very close to completing the building, said, 'Why didn't you tell me what it would look like?' And I said, 'Because I didn't know.'

It's probably like any work, whether a film or a book – it has its own inertia, it changes directions. Obviously you have to do

Name
Richard Rogers
Occupation
Architect
Company
Rogers Stirk
Harbour +
Partners
Location
His office,
London
Date
July 2013

working drawings, which you can't change very easily, but the scale changes. The scale in the models slowly gets more in tune with what you are actually doing and has, itself, a reaction to what you are doing. You can't imagine the finished 500 pages of a book and you can't imagine a finished building. Process is very important to me.

I was an appalling student all my life. In fact I often say I've enjoyed myself much more in the last third of my life than in the first third, which was hell – I was an Italian arriving in 1939 in England. That was a bad move to start with. Everybody said I was stupid, but then I found out I share my mother's dyslexia. That gave me a lot of problems for the first 30 years, but the last 30 years have been fantastic.

Above
The Centre Pompidou, Paris, by Richard Rogers and Renzo Piano

Richard Rogers

RR It was a competition for a museum, library, music centre and design centre in the centre of Paris, but a very rundown area. When we did our first studies, it showed that there was no public space nearby. So we created this big piazza. There were, I think, 681 entries and strangely enough there were no others with a big piazza.

The piazza is critical to the workings of the Pompidou. The idea was that you had a horizontal public space and you'd travel up the facade of the building in 'streets' in the air with escalators floating across them, so the whole thing became dynamic. People come to see people as well as to see art – people come to meet people. So we wanted to practice that as theatre. And on the facade, in the early proposals, was an electronic screen that could connect with any other museum or cultural centre.

What Renzo and I hadn't worked out was, of course, that the French are fantastic at promenading, so they promenaded through the piazza and then all these other people came.

Nobody said one kind word about the building until it opened, and then people started to queue up. I remember once standing outside on a rainy day and there was a small woman with an umbrella who offered me shelter. I accepted and we started talking, as one does in the rain, and she asked me, 'What do you

'We wanted to make a building that was clearly of our period, which caught the zeitgeist of the now'

think of this building?' Stupidly, which I would never normally do, I told her that I designed it, and she hit me on the head with her umbrella.

It was just typical of the general reaction of the people, especially during the design and construction stage: destroying their beautiful Paris. On the other hand, all good architecture is modern in its time. Gothic was a fantastic shock; the Renaissance was another shock to all the little medieval buildings. I come from Florence. The Palazzo Strozzi is eight storeys, and there's a famous document of one of the neighbours saying, 'Your building is completely out of scale.' Of course, from one storey to eight storeys is a big difference. The shock of the new is always rather difficult to get over, though it has got better. But boy, was that hard.

MF How did you and Renzo start working together?

RR Renzo and I are very close friends. We met about two years before we did the Pompidou and now we speak at least once a week and go sailing together. So we are very close; it's quite difficult to divide us. If you look at our earlier work, the house in Wimbledon for my parents, for example, which is a single-storey house, it's steel and highly insulated, it's transparent, the bathroom is compact and all the partitions can move... You can see a link from that to the Pompidou, with the difference being about a thousand times the scale. We wanted to make a building that was clearly of our period, which caught the zeitgeist of the now.

MF How did you come up with the design of the Pompidou? It was the late 1960s, a period of wild experimentation.

RR The big thing in those days was student movements, and it is said in France that Georges Pompidou[1] thought he'd lost the war against the students, workers and intellectuals. That moment nearly changed history, certainly for Europe. It looked as though there would be a revolution. It didn't happen, but we captured some of that in the building.

The facade, if you look more carefully, was very much about the riots and Vietnam. I met my wife through our friends who were escaping the draft – not that she was, but her friends were. It was a highly active period of politics. And you could argue that was part of the concept. Having said that, we rationalised it like hell.

If you look at the written documents, they very much tell you about the building. We said we'd put the building not in the middle of the piazza but actually to one side, because that will give people a place to meet. And then we'll put it on the street, so we can keep the nature of the long street. We need a movement system that is dynamic – I hate going up in internal lifts with people's heads in my stomach or vice versa. Why not give them a view? Movement should be celebrated.

So we had those concepts. There were the Metabolists[2] in Japan who were working, there was Archigram[3] in England. Those were different influences. The piazza in Siena – I don't even think we realised we'd done a piazza that was sloping a bit like it, but of course Siena must have been in our minds, as many others were. So the whole idea of Pompidou was as a place for the meeting of all people. The success of it was that the French took it over and it became the most visited building in Europe.

MF How did it relate to war and Vietnam?

RR The digital screen on the facade... At one level, if you looked at the proposal, was all about connections with culture. If you looked there, you'd see Vietnam, which was the dominant battle of the left. Whether you're writing it or building it, those moments are absorbed into those structures.

In a sense it comes back to this exhibition, which is trying to express not just my architecture but the fact that I believe architecture is political, that we have a social responsibility. What architects bring to architecture is a democratisation of the brief. The brief might be 60 floors of office space – which I can promise you is very boring as an architect – and the architect brings to it the possibility of having a forest on the roof, or having mixed work-leisure in that tower. The architect tries to humanise that tower so that not only the user but the viewer and the city are enriched, which ties back to the Athenian oath I mentioned earlier.

MF So the Pompidou was a product of 1960s radicalism?

RR The Pompidou was radical. I don't think we set out to create a radical building any more than a high-tech building. Those are titles that others, critics usually, attach to you. We may use them because they can explain a certain concept. But you don't sit down and think, 'I'm going to make it radical.'

MF Your next major project was the Lloyd's building in London.

RR We took about seven years to build the Pompidou. We had many political problems. We were taken to court regularly for a law saying that foreigners couldn't design cultural buildings for France, a law that had been written in the fascist era that nobody had thought to undo. The good thing was that Renzo and I, being in our thirties, were very naïve and didn't realise it was impossible, and so we carried on. But at the end of it there was no other work. Nobody wanted another Pompidou.

I went to teach in the States, my closest partner John Young thought about becoming a taxi driver and Renzo set up a small firm in France and had a tiny bit of work. I didn't really want to teach, I have to tell you.

Then there was a competition for Lloyd's. Lloyd's had one person on the board who had heard of the Royal Institute of British Architects, and we won their competition. It was truly different. If we were building more or less a fun palace in Paris, then this was a club. Lloyd's started in 1760 in a coffee house where financiers met sailors and captains and they did transactions. So it was very traditional. The only bit of technology when we went to see the existing building was a Xerox machine. Some people were still writing with quills and ink. Of course, it was the most famous insurance firm in the world and obviously contained a very cutting-edge element, but we were certainly strange bedfellows.

We were again extremely fortunate, in the same way that we had been with the Pompidou. The critical thing is having a good client. A good client is not somebody who just says 'yes'. It's a client that is engaged in the evolution of the building, who responds with 'no' at times because you can find another way of

doing it. The really difficult client is the sort that says, 'I don't mind what you do, I'll leave it to you,' and at the end says 'no'.

We were heavily engaged with Lloyd's. We spent half a day every month with the entire board of the company to discuss every part of the process. We were able to convince Lloyd's that we would put the mechanical services on the outside. Because mechanical services have a short life – they're like the engine of a car. Buildings have hundreds of years of life, streets have thousands of years of life. What needs changing is the air conditioning. Lloyd's said they wanted two things: they wanted a building that would last into the next century, because they'd built four buildings in about 50 years, and they wanted a building that could meet their changing needs.

Richard Rogers

The ducts and pieces on the outside allowed us to play a game with light and shadow. We brought big service towers upward, so you saw all these elements, which enrich the skyline of wonderful spires, towers and domes. Ours was a much more spiky building, and we were able to get this play of light and shadow in such a way that when we went to Blackheath or Parliament Hill to see how the light and shadow would play, the building was much more contextual; it had a greater sense of place than the Pompidou.

So we managed to persuade Lloyd's and Lloyd's managed to persuade us in such a way that we moved very well together. The other unspoken hero was Peter Rice[4], who joined us on the Pompidou and was a brilliant engineer. He guided us like a philosopher as well as a technologist. He was Irish and had clearly kissed the Blarney Stone. He could persuade us in the most wonderful and quiet way. Unfortunately he died of cancer in 1992. He was a great guy.

Before the building opened we were attacked by everybody. There was an investigation by the Bank of England into what was going on at Lloyd's, so the chairman had to resign. The next chairman hated us, so we had a very tough last year.

When the Queen opened the building I sat down next to the Dean of St Paul's Cathedral and he asked me, 'Do you feel beleaguered?' and I said, 'Yes, I'm being attacked on all sides by the press.' And he told me this story about Christopher Wren that I think we should all remember. Wren was in his seventies when he at last got to see St Paul's complete. He had started 30 years earlier and was so tired of having his building attacked and turned down, by the time he finished he put a six-metre wattle fence all around the site, so nobody could see it. Even St Paul's brought the shock of the new. We think it's been there forever – certainly Prince Charles thinks it has been there forever – but it hasn't and it was a risky building to build in those times. That's why it's great.

MF What do you think of the high-tech label that has been applied to your work?

RR Like Renzo, I have no great love for high-tech, but let me explain something. We do believe in the process of construction. Lloyd's was built in concrete with steel on the outside and the Pompidou was built in steel. Our Barajas airport in Madrid has wooden ceilings. I suppose one would like to think one uses the appropriate materials, but of course appropriate materials are also shaped by the time you live in, where you live and the machinery you are using. When you look at the beauty of cameras, watches and so on, the time certainly influences those.

The same thing happened in the fifteenth century. They were influenced by what was happening at that time: by perspective, which was invented in the fourteenth century, which clearly influenced how their buildings were designed. So we use the technology of today where appropriate to build the buildings of today. Then people say, 'Well, it's technology and therefore it's a high-tech building.' It sounds a bit too obvious.

MF So bring us up to date. Your most high-profile project today is the Leadenhall Building – the 'Cheesegrater' – near the Lloyd's building in the City of London.

RR The Leadenhall Building is the tallest in the City of London and Renzo's Shard is the tallest building in western Europe, so there we are again. Firstly, it's an office building and they tend to be very boring. One of the arts of architecture is not only to humanise but also to use the constraints. The main constraint with the Leadenhall was the view to St Paul's. London is unique in being partly controlled by protected views. You have to leave certain views open to St Paul's, and we were on one of those views. The only way to create a tall building was to slope out of that. So we cut it back at an angle. That gave us that prominent section and profile. We also had a client, again, that we got on with very well. British Land was willing to have a seven-storey public space below the building, a real public space. It won't have walls.

The building itself expresses its system of construction because we celebrate construction – it's one of the things in which we get scale and scale is a critical part. Architecture is about scale, about rhythm, about poetry, about geometry, obviously about

'It's exciting to see the dialogue between Lloyd's, Leadenhall and St Paul's. The enjoyment comes from that contrast'

beauty. Scale is how you recognise size as well as light and shadow. Height and length have limited use. You can make a building immensely large and overbearing that is a single storey or you can make a building that is very light with 50 storeys.

What's interesting for me is that whereas we thought Lloyd's was the absolute ultimate in technology, when I look at it now, it's practically handmade. Leadenhall was nearly all built off-site. The structure is less exposed. The shape is very important. The public space is very important. You can see the wonderful banks of elevators, toilets and so on, what we will call the back. So the elements that we've got to know well, we're using there. But in a

Richard Rogers

1 Georges
Pompidou was
president of
France from
1969 until his
death in 1974.
The Centre
Pompidou was
named after him

2 The postwar
Japanese
Metabolism
movement
approached
buildings and
cities as living,
organically
evolving entities

3 Archigram was
an avant-garde
architecture
group formed
in London in
the 1960s, which
explored radical,
hypothetical
visions of
technologically
advanced future
cities

4 Peter Rice was
a structural
engineer with the
global engineering
firm Arup

way, more or less 40 years later, it's all machine made, and the
next one will be even more so.

It's exciting to see the dialogue between Lloyd's, Leadenhall
and the dome of St Paul's, built in a totally different period. To me,
that's what architecture is all about. It's not about fitting it in, it's
setting up these dialogues. The enjoyment of St Paul's was that
it was seen against the low and rather poor medieval background.
So it's a beauty that comes from contrast.

MF What would you describe as the greatest achievement of your
career to date?

RR I have a terrific family. I have a wonderful wife, who is a chef, so
I can eat every day in the River Café, one of the best Italian
restaurants in this part of the world. That's probably my number
one pride. I'm proud of the fact that I've been very fortunate to
work with lots of fantastic colleagues. I've changed the name of
the firm to Rogers Stirk Harbour + Partners because of the
contribution the partners have made, and at 80 I can see an end
will be coming. But I would like to think my ethos may continue.

We have a constitution where the partners gave up their
ownership of the company. We're now owned by a charity. We
only do certain types of work and that has created a sense of
team spirit. So I'm proud of those things and I'm proud of the
fact that I've been able to live at a time when I've been able to
make use of my abilities.

MF What one change would you wish for in architecture?

RR On one side Britain now has very good modern architects, and
you could argue no nation has better. The Pritzker Prize, which is
sometimes spoken about as the Nobel Prize for architecture
– there are probably more English architects with Pritzkers than
anywhere else except Japan. So the architecture is there. Political
interest has never been much but it is greater.

If you go to the City of London, it's pretty good now. I was
coming out of the Design Museum recently, on the other side of
Tower Bridge, and looking at the skyline I thought I was in New
York, with all the towers and lights. It's exciting, dynamic and
something that was impossible before.

I think what has gone is our social role. In my generation
every architect who left school went to work for the school
department, the hospital department, the housing department,
the local county council and so on. I'm going to say 90 percent
of the students with me at the Architecture Association wanted to
build a better future. This has gone and it is much more an age of
greed. There's an acceptance that it doesn't matter what you earn,
you have no duty to society, and I think that's reflected in some
of the things we do. I often point out Finland, where teachers get
the same money as surgeons because they are recognised for their
important role.

But it's a very exciting time and now we're looking at an international world. We weren't when I started. Now we can make use of a much wider network of communication and change and adapt to that network. I wouldn't say things are uglier than they were, but we have to be wary of protecting the public realm.

Above
The Leadenhall Building, London, by Rogers Stirk Harbour + Partners

Isabelle Olsson
'A firefighter developed an app to see the floorplan of a building, so Glass can help save lives'

We spoke to the Swedish industrial designer, who joined Google's X Lab in 2011, about how she set about designing desirable frames for the wearable computer Google Glass.

James Pallister How did you start designing Google Glass?

Isabelle Olsson I had a very simple, concise brief and it was to make this prototype of Google Glass beautiful and comfortable. When I first joined I had no idea what I was going to work on. I just knew I was joining Google X and working on something new and exciting. Then I walked into a room full of engineers wearing a prototype of the glasses: 3D-printed frames with a cellphone battery strapped to the legs. They weighed about 200 grams.

JP What were your initial design intentions?

IO My initial goal was, 'How do we make these incredibly light?' I set up three design principles; if you have something that is very complex, you need to stick to some principles. The first was lightness, the second was simplicity and the third was scalability.

The first thing that made me nervous was not, 'How are we going to make this technology work?' but, 'How will we make this work for people? How are we going to make people want to wear the glasses?' The first thing that came to mind is that when you walk into a glasses store you see hundreds of styles. From the very beginning we designed this to be modular and to evolve over time. There is this tiny screw that is meant to be screwed off, and then you can remove the frame and attach different kinds of frames.

JP You're launching new prescription frames and sunglasses, which fit the Google Glass you launched in 2013.

IO Yes. This is our first collection of new frames. The frames are accessories, so you detach the really expensive and complex technology from the style part. You can have a couple of different frames and you don't need to get another Glass device. So we're finally starting to let people wear what they want to wear.

JP How many people were on the team that refined the clunky prototype into what we see today?

IO The team started off very small: it was like a little science project. As we started to transition it into something you could actually wear, we have grown the team. Our design team is still really small – I can count them on my fingers.

JP What kind of people do you have on your team?

IO I really believe in having a mixed team: graphic designers, interior designers, design strategists and industrial designers, but also

Name
Isabelle Olsson
Occupation
Industrial designer
Company
Google X Lab
Location
New York, via Google Hangout
Date
January 2014

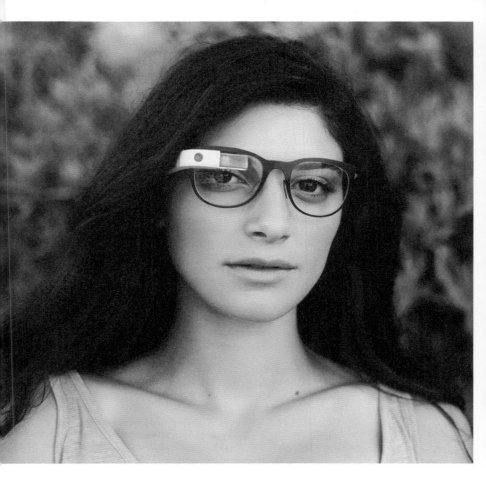

people who work in the fashion industry. The funny thing is almost nobody on the design team has a technology background, which is unusual for a tech company. But the great thing about it is it keeps us grounded and keeps us thinking about it from a lifestyle standpoint.

JP Is that one of the strengths of the team, that you're not too obsessed with the technology?

IO There's often the view that designers and engineers have to fight, that there should be a constant battle. I don't believe that. I think that view belongs in the 1990s.

JP Are the glasses manufactured by Google?

IO They're made in Japan. They are made of beautiful titanium that is extremely lightweight and durable.

Above
A model wearing one of the new frames designed for Google Glass

Isabelle Olsson

1 'Explorer' is
the term given
to early adopters
who have been
given access
to Google Glass

JP **With the spectacles and sunglasses, how did you choose which styles to develop?**

IO There actually aren't that many styles out there, so we looked at the most popular and condensed them into iconic, simplified versions. Bold, for example, is great for people who would normally prefer a chunky, square style. Curve is a bit more fashion-forward. And Split is for those who like almost rimless glasses, that are lighter on your face. Thin is a classic, simple style that doesn't stand out.

JP **Had you ever designed glasses before?**

IO I've designed glasses and jewellery, so it wasn't completely new. But we did spend a long time refining these. We wanted the shape to be absolutely perfect. A two-millimetre height difference makes a complete difference to the way it looks on your face. Prototyping was absolutely crucial. We also cut paper and used laser-cutting and 3D printing.

JP **What was the design process?**

IO We would start with sketching by hand, then with Illustrator or a 2D programme. Then we would laser-cut these shapes in paper and do alterations. Next we would go into a harder material, like plastic. Once we had the icons, we 3D-printed those. Then we got into laser-cutting metals. So it was a long back-and-forth process.

JP **So it was quite a manual process?**

IO Yes. What looks good on the computer doesn't necessarily translate, especially with something that goes on your face. As soon as you have an idea, you need to prototype it to see what is broken about it. You can then see what looks weird. It can be completely off – too big or too nerdy – and look crazy. It can be a case of a couple of millimetres.

The next stage is about trying it on people, because something like this needs to fit a wide range of people. That's what I think is most exciting: that everyone on our team uses Glass now. We gave them prototypes early on. It was so interesting to get feedback from them and valuable for me to see people walking around with them every day.

JP **What do people pay for the device?**

IO The Explorer edition, the version of Glass released last year, is now $1500. The new prescription-glass accessory will be $225.

JP **Did you have to build different software to cope with the curvature of the lens?**

IO No, it works with the regular device. What's great about it is that our existing Explorers[1] can buy the accessory, just the frame, and then attach it to their device.

JP **How long do you think it will be before wearing Google Glass becomes a normal, everyday thing? Five years? Ten years?**

IO Much sooner than ten years, I'd say. The technology keeps evolving. That's the critical part about the Explorer programme – to get people using Glass in their daily lives. Once more people have it, they'll get used to it faster. Even with the original edition or the base frame: after half an hour, people forget they're wearing it, it's so lightweight. Then it's about the people around you getting used to it. That takes maybe three times the amount of time.

JP Have you heard of any unexpected uses of Glass?

IO I was hoping for these cases, so when something comes up I'm more excited than surprised. The artistic uses appeal to me as a designer, when people use it to make stop-motion videos or other art projects. But also there's this firefighter who developed an app so he can see the floorplan of a building, so it could help save lives. The more people I see using it, the more exciting it gets and the more diverse it becomes.

JP It seems that we're getting closer and closer to a circumstance where we can record every situation. Does that ever worry you from a privacy viewpoint?

IO I think with any new technology you need to develop an etiquette for using it. When cellphones started having cameras on them,

'A two-millimetre height difference makes a complete difference to the way it looks on your face'

people freaked out. Part of the Explorer programme is hearing how Glass is working, when it's useful and in what instances you use it. We're also interested in the social side: how people react when you're wearing it. What are people's concerns, fears, issues and hopes for it? We hope Glass will help people interact with the world around them, quickly process information and move on to the conversation they were having.

JP What's the next stage for Glass?

IO Right now we are focused on slowly growing the Explorer programme, making sure people get these frames in their hands – or on their faces, I should say. We are really excited about that, but obviously we are prioritising feedback and creating next-generation products that I can't talk about!

JP Are there any types of technology you think Glass will feed into in the future?

IO It's hard for us to speculate without revealing things, but the focus is to make technology a more natural part of you. Glass is going to feed into that.

Image credits

Ron Arad
Portrait by Oliver Manzi © Dezeen
Rover chair © Ron Arad Associates
Tom Vac chair © Tom Vack, courtesy of Ron Arad Associates

Hella Jongerius
Portrait by Oliver Manzi © Dezeen
KLM interior © KLM

Neri&Hu
Portraits by Oliver Manzi © Dezeen
Interior of Design Republic Commune © Pedro Pegenaute

Yves Béhar
Portrait by Oliver Manzi © Dezeen
BIG Jambox © Fuseproject and Jawbone

Ilse Crawford
Portrait © Stef Bakker, courtesy of Studioilse
Grand Hôtel interior © Magnus Marding, courtesy of Studioilse

Ben Terrett
Portrait by Oliver Manzi © Dezeen

Julian Hakes
Portrait by Peer Lindgreen © Julian Hakes Associates
Mojito shoe photographed by Tyson Sadlo © Julian Hakes Associates

Neville Brody
Portrait © Research Studios
23 Skidoo album cover © Research Studios

David Adjaye
Portrait by Oliver Manzi © Dezeen
Adjaye Africa Architecture © David Adjaye Associates

Piet Hein Eek
Portrait by Alice Masters © Dezeen
Waste Waste 40×40 © Nob Ruijgrok, courtesy of Studio Piet Hein Eek

Wim Crouwel
Portraits by Luke Hayes © Design Museum

Craig Robins
Portrait and Cardozo hotel photographed by Oliver Manzi © Dezeen

Thomas Heatherwick
Portrait by Oliver Manzi © Dezeen
UK Pavilion at Shanghai Expo 2010 © Iwan Baan

Winy Maas
Portrait © Boudewijn Bollmann, courtesy of MVRDV
Balancing Barn exterior and interior © Edmund Sumner, courtesy of MVRDV and Living Architecture

Alexandra Daisy Ginsberg
Portrait by Oliver Manzi © Dezeen
Slug-like bioremediating device © Alexandra Daisy Ginsberg

Paul Smith
Portrait by Oliver Manzi © Dezeen

Arik Levy
Portrait © Arik Levy
Transition collection for Kolon Sport photographed by A.Salazar © Arik Levy

Marc Newson
Portrait by Oliver Manzi © Dezeen
Ford O21C Concept car © Tom Vack, courtesy of Marc Newson

Neri Oxman
Portrait by Jane Messinger © Dezeen

Kieran Long
Portrait by Ben Hobson © Dezeen
Liberator gun © Cody Wilson / Defense Distributed

Barber&Osgerby
Portraits by Oliver Manzi © Dezeen
London 2012 Olympic Torch © Barber & Osgerby

Peter Zumthor
Portrait by Hufton and Crow © Serpentine Galleries
Serpentine Gallery Pavilion 2011 photographed by Hufton and Crow © Serpentine Galleries

Tom Dixon
Portrait by Oliver
Manzi © Dezeen
Flame Cut Series
chair © Mitterrand
+ Cramer

Iris van Herpen
Portrait by Marc
de Groot © Dezeen
Crystallization
3D-printed
garment © Duy Vo

Oki Sato
Portrait by Oliver
Manzi © Dezeen
Camper store
© Daici Ano,
courtesy of Nendo

Tim Kobe
Portrait by Oliver
Manzi © Dezeen

Rem Koolhaas
Portrait by
Dominik Gigler
© OMA
De Rotterdam
building © Ossip
van Duivenbode,
courtesy of
Rotterdam
Partners

Imogen Heap
Portrait by Marcus
Fairs © Dezeen
Mi.Mu. glove
© Adrian Lausch

Dietmar Thomas
Portrait by Oliver
Manzi © Dezeen
LivingShapes
interactive
wall © Philips
Lumiblade

Hussein Chalayan
Portrait © Chris
Moore, courtesy
of Chalayan

Formafantasma
Portraits by Alice
Masters © Dezeen
Botanica vase
© Luisa Zanzani,
courtesy of
Formafantasma

Suzanne Lee
Portrait by Ben
Hobson © Dezeen
BioSkirt 2014
photographed by
House Of Radon
© BioCouture

Patrick Seguin
Portrait © Galerie
Patrick Seguin
Maison
Démontable 8 × 8
© Galerie Patrick
Seguin

Job Smeets
Portrait by Oliver
Manzi © Dezeen
Bucket Floor Lamp
© Moooi, courtesy
of Studio Job

Sadie Morgan
Portrait by Ben
Hobson © Dezeen
Battersea Power
Station housing
development
© Battersea
Power Station
Development
Company,
courtesy of dRMM

Naoto Fukasawa
Portrait by Oliver
Manzi © Dezeen
Papilio bed
© B&B Italia

David Chipperfield
Portrait © Ingrid
von Kruse,
courtesy of David
Chipperfield
Architects
Wall House
© Andreas Deffner,
courtesy of
Anupama Kundoo

Janne Kyttanen
Portrait by Oliver
Manzi © Dezeen

Paul Priestman
Portrait by Oliver
Manzi © Dezeen
Mercury train
high speed train
© Priestmangoode

Sou Fujimoto
Portrait by Oliver
Manzi © Dezeen
Serpentine Gallery
Pavilion 2013
© Iwan Baan

Andy Millns
Portrait by Oliver
Manzi © Dezeen
Oculus Rift
© Inition
Augmented reality
app © Inition /
Drees and Sommer

Konstantin Grcic
Portrait by Oliver
Manzi © Dezeen
Design Real
installation view
© Raphael Hefti,
courtesy of
Serpentine Galleries

James Dyson
Portrait © Dyson

Richard Rogers
Portrait by Oliver
Manzi © Dezeen
Centre Pompidou
© Katsuhisa Kida
Lloyd's building
© Richard Bryant
The Leadenhall
Building
© British Land

Isabelle Olsson
Portrait
© Google Inc.
Google Glass
© Google Inc.

Index

About Dezeen

Dezeen was launched by Marcus Fairs in November 2006 and grew rapidly to become the world's most influential online architecture and design magazine.

From the outset it had a simple mission: to publish a carefully curated selection of cutting-edge architecture, interiors and design projects.

Dezeen has now grown beyond the original magazine into a family of sites serving designers and design-savvy consumers around the world, and includes the Dezeen Jobs recruitment site and the Dezeen Watch Store timepiece boutique.

Collectively the sites attract around two million unique visitors every month, and this figure is growing all the time.

Dezeen Book of Interviews is Dezeen's second paper-based publication, following the success of Dezeen Book of Ideas, which was published in 2011.

The book has been designed by Micha Weidmann Studio.